Intelligent Business

Skills Book

Rachel Appleby

Intermediate Business English

| Christine Johnson | Irene Barrall |

Pearson Education Limited
Edinburgh Gate
Harlow
Essex CM20 2JE
England
and Associated Companies throughout the world.

www.longman.com

© Pearson Education Limited 2006

The right of Christine Johnson and Irene Barrall to be identified as authors of this Work has been asserted by them in accordance with the Copyright, Designs and Patents Act 1988.

All rights reserved; no part of this publication may be reproduced, stored in a retrieval system, or transmitted in any form or by any means, electronic, mechanical, photocopying, recording, or otherwise without the prior written permission of the Publishers.

First published 2006

Intelligent Business Upper-Intermediate Skills Book for pack.
ISBN-13: 978-0-582-84806-1
ISBN-10: 0-582-84806-7

Intelligent Business Upper-Intermediate Skills Book and CD-ROM pack.
ISBN-13: 978-0-582-84696-8
ISBN-10: 0-582-84696-x

Set in Economist Roman 10.5 / 12.5

Printed in Spain by Graficas Estella

Acknowledgements
The authors would like to thank Tony Garside and Stephen Nicholl for their excellent editorial support.

The publishers would like to thank the following people for their helpful comments on the manuscript for this book: Louise Bulloch, Intercom Language Services GmbH; Steve Bush, The British Institute, Florence; William Cooley, Open Schools of Languages, Madrid; Peter Dunn, Groupe ESC, Dijon, Bourgogne; Jolanta Korc-Migoń, Warsaw University of Technology, Louise Pile, UK.

The publishers would like to thank the following people for their help in piloting and developing this course: Richard Booker and Karen Ngeow, University of Hong Kong; Adolfo Escuder, EU Estudios Empresariales, University of Zaragoza; Wendy Farrar, Università Cattolica del Sacro Cuore, Piacenza; Andrew Hopgood, Linguarama, Hamburg; Ann-Marie Hadzima, Dept of Foreign Languages, National Taiwan University, Taiwan; Samuel C. M. Hsieh, English Department, Chinese Culture University, Taipei; Laura Lewis, ABS International, Buenos Aires; Maite Padrós, Universitat de Barcelona; Giuliete Aymard Ramos Siqueira, São Paulo; Richmond Stroupe, World Language Center, Soka University, Tokyo; Michael Thompson, Centro Linguistico Università Commerciale L. Bocconi, Milan; Krisztina Tüll, Európai Nyelvek Stúdiója, Budapest.

Photo Acknowledgements
The publishers are grateful to the following for their permission to reproduce copyright photographs.

Alamy/Camelot p1(r), p34, Rob Crandall p65; Corbis/Brownie Harris p17, Yang Liu p20(bl), Jose Luis Pelaez Inc p35, p44, p54, p67, p70, William Taufic p36, Royalty Free p42; Ford Motor Company/Jaguar p59; Getty Images/VEER p13, Karen Moskowitz p14, White Packert p24, Phil Boorman p39, Stewart Cohen p50, Walter Hodges p52, Tim Brown p56, Ron Chapple p58, Frank Herholdt p62, Tony May p64, The Moment p68, Rich LaSalle p71; nTAG Interactive (www.ntag.com) p7; Punchstock p6, /Digital Vision p38, p1(c), p66; Rex Features/AXV p22; Superstock/Javier Larrea p9, ILA2 p1(l), p10, ITA Stock (Royalty Free) p20(t), Zave Smith p20(br), p26, David Muscroft p28, Don Klumpp p48.

Every effort has been made to trace the copyright holders and we apologise in advance for any unintentional omissions. We would be pleased to insert the appropriate acknowledgement in any subsequent edition of this publication.

Front cover images supplied by Alamy/Camelot (r), Punchstock (c), Superstock/ILA2 (l).

Picture Research by Liz Moore.

Illustrated by John Bradley

Designed by Neil Straker Creative

Contents

Intelligent Business Upper Intermediate

Unit 1
Break the ice
In this unit you will practise starting a conversation and making small talk. You will also have the chance to look at polite conversational responses and ask open and closed questions. **Page 6.**

Introduction

6 **Unit 1**
Break the ice

10 **Unit 2**
Make a strong start

14 **Unit 3**
Build the team

18 **Writing 1**
Emails

20 **Unit 4**
Ask questions

24 **Unit 5**
Present facts and figures

28 **Unit 6**
Entertain guests

32 **Writing 2**
Factual reports

34 **Unit 7**
Bid and bargain

38 **Unit 8**
Chair a meeting

42 **Unit 9**
Emphasise your point

46 **Writing 3**
Memos

48 **Unit 10**
Manage a crisis

52 **Unit 11**
Adapt to your audience

56 **Unit 12**
Make a difficult call

60 **Writing 4**
Formal correspondence

62 **Unit 13**
Get to yes

66 **Unit 14**
Sell your idea

70 **Unit 15**
Summarise

74 **Writing 5**
Minutes

76 **Good business practice**

83 **Grammar reference**

97 **Pairwork**

105 **Audioscripts**

Unit 7
Bid and bargain
In this unit you will have the chance to role-play two negotiating situations. You will also practise making proposals and counter proposals, and bargaining for agreement. **Page 34.**

On the inside back cover of this book you will find an interactive CDROM with extra activities, audio files and clips from the **Intelligent Business Upper Intermediate Video.** There is also a reference section with grammar, culture notes and good business practice.

Unit 10
Manage a crisis
This unit will help you to prepare an action plan to identify and deal with a potential crisis. You will also look at phrases to talk about possible solutions to a problem and then hold a crisis meeting **Page 48.**

From the authors

The *Intelligent Business Upper Intermediate Skills Book* provides a practical approach to developing each of the core business skills: presentations, attending and leading meetings, negotiating, socialising and telephoning.

The book is for upper intermediate learners who are either already in work, or studying and preparing for a career in business.

How can the book be used?

The Skills Book provides all the components for a complete course. However, it can also be used in conjunction with the *Intelligent Business Upper Intermediate Coursebook*. Each Skills Book unit gives further practice of language introduced in the equivalent coursebook units. There is also an *Intelligent Business Upper Intermediate Video* that shows the language and business skills common to both books in practice.

The Skills Book can be taught as a one-week intensive course of 30 contact hours; or it can be used for classes that attend once or twice a week over a longer period. It is designed for groups of four to eight students, but can be adapted for use with larger groups, or with one-to-one students. (See *Intelligent Business Upper Intermediate Teacher's Book* for guidelines.)

What is in the units?

Each unit contains two or three practical speaking tasks, which are designed to develop the skills you need to meet the objectives of the unit. After each task, you will have a short analysis session, which will help you to evaluate your performance. There are also listening activities in each unit, which provide a model of key language and will also help you to develop your listening skills.

The section *What do you think?* gives you the chance to discuss your own experience of business. If you don't have any experience of work, you can refer to the *Good business practice* section at the back of the book. The culture notes will help you to find out how other cultures approach common business situations. You can draw up your own culture profile by completing the chart on page 82.

There are five writing units in the book which will give you practice in the kinds of writing that are essential to business: emails, factual reports, memos, formal correspondence and minutes of meetings. You can go to the *Grammar reference* for information about the main grammar points, and for exercises to help you practise key points.

The integrated CDROM will give you extra practice activities to do on your own. You can practise listening to the dialogues from each unit and watch short extracts from the *Intelligent Business Upper Intermediate Video*.

We hope you enjoy using this book and find it helpful in improving your English. Good luck!

Christine Johnson and Irene Barrall

Bookmap

90-120 minute block					
	Unit 1 Break the ice ■ 6 Start a conversation Make small talk	**Unit 4** Ask questions ■ 20 Prepare questions Ask for factual information Find out about needs and interests	**Unit 7** Bid and bargain ■ 34 Make proposals and counter-proposals Bargain for agreement	**Unit 10** Manage a crisis ■ 48 Prepare an action plan Hold a crisis meeting	**Unit 13** Get to yes ■ 62 Make the most of your position Reach agreement

90-120 minute block					
	Unit 2 Make a strong start ■ 10 Give a short introduction Stimulate interest Prepare an introduction	**Unit 5** Present facts and figures ■ 24 Present figures accurately Analyse information	**Unit 8** Chair a meeting ■ 38 Control a meeting Deal with people effectively	**Unit 11** Adapt to your audience ■ 52 Use informal language Simplify and explain	**Unit 14** Sell your idea ■ 66 Present a proposal Make a strong conclusion

90-120 minute block					
	Unit 3 Build the team ■ 14 Make a contribution Play an active role	**Unit 6** Entertain guests ■ 28 Guide a conversation Tell a story	**Unit 9** Emphasise your point ■ 42 Emphasise priorities Make your point strongly	**Unit 12** Make a difficult call ■ 56 Resolve a misunderstanding Handle conflict	**Unit 15** Summarise ■ 70 Summarise points Give an accurate report

| | **Writing 1**
Emails
■ 18
Make a strong start
Be friendly and diplomatic | **Writing 2**
Factual reports
■ 32
Write an executive summary | **Writing 3**
Memos
■ 46
Organise the information
Write a clear proposal | **Writing 4**
Formal correspondence
■ 60
Write a follow-up letter to a telephone call
Write a formal letter | **Writing 5**
Minutes
■ 74
Record key information
Record decisions and actions |

Good business practice
■ 76

Grammar reference
■ 83

Pairwork
■ 97

Audioscripts
■ 105

Unit 14
Sell your idea

In this unit you will prepare arguments and practise presenting a proposal. You will also practise bringing your proposal to a strong conclusion. **Page 66.**

Unit 1 | Break the ice

| Start a conversation | Make small talk |

Task 1

Objective: Start a conversation

Boston-based company nTAG have designed a conference badge with a difference: delegates enter information about their jobs and interests. When they meet another person with similar hobbies, the interactive badges introduce the wearers and tell them what they have in common. The aim is to make networking easier by using the badge to help start conversations.

Whole group
5 minutes

Step 1

What information would you put on your nTAG badge? Make a badge for yourself and include information about:

– your job
– your interests outside work
– something interesting or surprising about who you are or what you do

Use no more than ten words for each topic.

Whole group
10 minutes

Step 2

Move around the room introducing yourself and shaking hands. Use the information on the badge to start a short conversation with each person. Talk to as many people as possible and move on to a new person after one or two minutes.

Analysis
5 minutes

Did you find it easy or difficult to start a conversation?
What did you find most difficult?
Did the badges help? How?
What did you talk about with different people?

What do you think? Whole group 5 minutes	### Breaking the ice Do you think the nTAG badge is a useful idea to help break the ice when starting a conversation? Imagine you are attending a conference where you don't know anyone. It is the first coffee break and lots of people are standing around talking. How would you start a conversation? What techniques can you think of to join in a conversation with a group of people? Would you use the same techniques to break the ice with an individual?

 Good business practice, page 76

What do you say?
5 minutes

Starting a conversation

There are several ways to start a conversation. Match the techniques 1–4 with the phrases a–d.

1 Greeting
2 Asking an open question
3 Making a statement
4 Using a tag question

a That was an interesting talk about managing change.
b The CEO is a brilliant speaker, isn't he?
c I don't think we've met – I'm …
d How are you enjoying the conference?

 Grammar reference: Review of tenses 1, Present tenses, page 83

 Grammar reference: Question forms, page 87

CD 2 Listening 1
5 minutes

Listen to the start of eight conversations and identify which technique above each speaker uses.

Practice
Pairs
5 minutes

Use the techniques in the following situations.

1 You are waiting to get your ID badge at the start of a conference. Think of something to say to the person waiting in front of you in the queue.
2 The first speaker has just finished their presentation. The speech went on for forty minutes longer than expected. Say something to the person sitting next to you.
3 There is a coffee break between talks. You are waiting to get a drink. Start a conversation with the person standing next to you.
4 You are in the self-service cafeteria at lunchtime. You think there's a free seat at one of the tables. Ask the person sitting at the table if the seat is free and start a conversation.
5 There is a party at the end of the conference. You see one of the speakers standing alone. Introduce yourself and start a conversation.

Unit 1 7

Culture at work

Making small talk

People have different areas of their life, which we can call 'life spaces'. Our personal or private life space is the part which we keep to ourselves, or share with our family and very close friends. Our public life space is the part that we are happy to share with the people we meet on a casual or short-term basis. People from specific cultures have a small private space and relatively large public space: those from diffuse cultures have a much larger private space. Which are you? Complete your culture profile on page 82.

People from specific cultures ...	People from diffuse cultures ...
seem friendly and accessible because they give information about themselves freely from the very first meeting.	seem hard to know because they don't tell you much about themselves unless they know you well.
have friendly relationships with a lot of people who are not necessarily close or lifetime friends. These relationships may seem superficial to people from diffuse cultures.	have a few close friends, with whom they have a long-term relationship and share many aspects of their private lives.
are happy to talk about personal matters with anyone they meet.	don't like to talk about personal matters in the context of a business relationship.

What do you say?
Pairs
10 minutes

Open and closed questions

Look at these conversational questions. Which are closed (can be answered with a simple Yes or No)? Which ones are open (more likely to lead to a longer response)?

1 Are you staying at this hotel?
2 What do you think of the hotel?
3 It's very informal here, isn't it?
4 Are you here on your own?
5 What are things like in your country?
6 What kind of business are you in?
7 Do you travel much in your job?
8 What do you like about travelling?

Use the prompts below to ask your partner questions.

Are you interested in ... ?
What do you think of ... ?
What are things like in your ... ?
What do you like about ... ?

CD 3 ⊙ Listening 2
10 minutes

1 Listen to six short conversations between people who have just met at a conference. In which conversations do people ask open questions?

2 Listen again and notice the responses. In which conversations do the people responding sound interested and friendly?

What do you say?
Pairs
5 minutes

Conversational responses

1 Look at the typical conversational responses 1–6 below. Think of a comment that could lead to each response.

2 Work with a different partner. Take turns to make your comments and respond with one of the phrases.

1 Oh, really?
2 That sounds good.
3 What a pity.
4 That's true, yes.
5 It is, isn't it?
6 How nice.

Task 2
Whole group
15–20 minutes

Objective: Make small talk

You are attending a welcome party on the first evening of a conference. Start a conversation with at least three other people. After a few minutes, stop the conversation and move on to someone new. Remember to:

- use open questions
- respond with interest
- use a polite phrase to move on, for example:

You'll have to excuse me a moment ...
It was good to meet you ...
I have to go now, but it was good talking to you ...

Analysis
5 minutes

Were you able to think of suitable ways of starting a conversation?
Were you able to respond to questions?
How did your partner show interest?
Did you find it easy or difficult to move on to the next person?

Self-assessment

Think about your performance on the tasks. Were you able to:

- start a conversation? ☐ yes ☐ need more practice
- make small talk? ☐ yes ☐ need more practice

Unit 2 | Make a strong start

| Give a short introduction | Stimulate interest | Prepare an introduction |

Task 1
Individually
5 minutes

Objective: Give a short introduction

Step 1 Preparation

Choose one of the topics below and prepare a short introduction to a presentation. Your introduction should take about one minute. Information about the context and content of the presentation are given at the back of the book. Alternatively, you can invent the details yourself.

Topic A: A new IT system, turn to page 97.
Topic B: Your company, turn to page 98.

You may want to use some of the following language.

*The purpose of this presentation is to ...
If you have any questions, please feel free to interrupt.
I'd like to bring you up to date on ...
I've divided my talk into three parts. First ...
The second point I'd like to consider is ...
And finally, I'll talk about ...*

Pairs
5 minutes

Step 2 Presentation

Work with a partner from the other group. Present your introduction to your partner. Listen to your partner's introduction and complete the form and checklist opposite.

1 Topic / Purpose of presentation: _____
2 Who do you think the audience might be? _____
3 What did your partner include in the introduction?
   ☐ A greeting
   ☐ His / Her name and job title
   ☐ The topic or purpose of the presentation
   ☐ A list of points to be covered in the presentation
   ☐ An instruction about when the audience can ask questions

Analysis
5 minutes

Did your partner make the topic and purpose of the presentation clear?
Did they greet the audience appropriately?
What did they include in their introduction? Was this enough?

What do you think?
Whole group
5 minutes

The goals of an introduction

Which of the following do you think are important goals for an introduction?

1 Give the topic of the presentation.
2 Prepare the audience for what is going to come.
3 Stimulate interest in what you have to say.
4 Make a connection with your audience and build a relationship with them.
5 Give yourself time to think what you want to say.
6 Make a good impression.
7 Give the audience time to settle down and get focused.
8 Other? _____

Good business practice, page 76

CD 4 Listening 1
15 minutes

1 Listen to two examples of introductions. Look at goals 1–4 above and decide if they were achieved by the introductions.

2 Listen again and tick strategies a–e below which each presenter used to stimulate interest in their topic.

		1	2
a	Refer to what the audience already knows.	☐	☐
b	Emphasise the importance of the topic for this audience.	☐	☐
c	Give an interesting fact or tell a story.	☐	☐
d	Ask a rhetorical question (one that doesn't need an answer) to introduce a point.	☐	☐
e	Ask a question that the audience should respond to.	☐	☐

Grammar reference: Articles, page 91

What do you say?	**Stimulating interest**
5 minutes	

Match each of the strategies 1–5 with two of the phrases a–j.

1 Refer to what the audience already knows.
2 Emphasise the importance of the topic for this audience.
3 Give an interesting fact or tell a story.
4 Ask a rhetorical question as a way of introducing a point.
5 Ask a question that the audience should respond to.

a As you know …
b It may surprise you to know that 90 per cent of people tell lies when they apply for a job.
c Anyone like to guess?
d As you are all involved in this project, you will need to know …
e So, what about costs?
f There's an interesting story about this …
g You may be familiar with the idea of …
h Raise your hand if you think it's a good idea to …
i This information is important for making a decision on …
j How can we improve communication between international teams?

Task 2	**Objective: Stimulate interest**
Pairs	**Step 1 Preparation**
5 minutes	

Read the introduction to a presentation which is aimed at a large group of town planners at an annual conference. You are going to help the presenter to make this introduction more exciting. You could use the additional information below. Discuss your ideas with a partner. You can change the order, add new phrases or questions or change the wording of the text. Be ready to demonstrate your new introduction to the rest of the group.

> The subject of my presentation is 'Planning for healthy living'. I'm going to outline some new approaches to planning the way we build suburban areas, which will help to improve people's health and lifestyle. My talk will cover three main points: first – planning for amenities such as shops, schools and sports facilities. Second – public transport. And third – safety: some strategies for reducing crime. The first point, then, is planning for amenities.

Additional information you could use in your introduction
- Research from the US: people who live in city centres are generally healthier than people who live in the suburbs.
- Suburban residents are more dependent on cars to get around, walk less, are more overweight and have higher blood pressure.
- Planners must consider how to encourage people to walk more.

Whole group	**Step 2 Presentation**
1 minute per pair	

One person from each pair should present their revised introduction to the group.

| CD 5 Listening 2
5 minutes | Listen to a new version of the introduction in Task 2 and compare it with your own.

1 Did the presenter organise his introduction in the same way as you?
2 Was his introduction surprising? Was it effective, in your opinion?
3 Did you have the same ideas for stimulating interest?
4 What differences in language did you notice? |

| Culture at work | **Attitudes to time**

People from different cultures have different concepts of time. In monochronic cultures, time is seen as a precious resource that must not be wasted. In synchronic cultures, people have a more flexible attitude to time. Which is closer to your culture? Complete your culture profile on page 82. |

	Monochronic	Synchronic
Planning events	Events are tightly scheduled and people expect each part of the event to start and finish at a precise time.	Although events have a timetable, people accept that the timing can change to allow for eventualities.
Planning presentations	Presenters plan each stage of their presentation carefully. Audiences may be critical of presentations that overrun.	Presenters prepare a plan but they may change it to adapt to the situation or the needs of the audience.
Introducing presentations	Introductions are usually short and to the point.	Presenters often take more time to build a relationship with the audience.

| Task 3 | **Objective: Prepare an introduction** |

| Individually
10–15 minutes | **Step 1 Preparation**

Choose a new topic for a presentation. It could be something related to your work or a general interest topic. Think of three or four points to cover. Then decide how you could make a strong start, one which creates an impact and stimulates audience interest. |

| Whole group
2 minutes per presentation | **Step 2 Presentation**

Present your introduction to the rest of the group. |

| Analysis
5 minutes | How did each introduction create an impact?
Did the presenter ask the audience to participate in any way?
What other strategies did the presenter use to stimulate interest in the topic? |

| Self-assessment | Think about your performance on the tasks. Were you able to:

- give a short introduction?   ☐ yes   ☐ need more practice
- stimulate interest?   ☐ yes   ☐ need more practice
- prepare an introduction?   ☐ yes   ☐ need more practice |

Unit 3 | Build the team

| Make a contribution | Play an active role |

Task 1
Groups of 4–6
10 minutes

Objective: Make a contribution

You are all members of a newly-formed international team which will share ideas for marketing activities. Each of you is the marketing manager in a different country. You are all of equal status in the organisational hierarchy. Hold an initial meeting to cover the agenda below. Everyone should make a contribution to the meeting. Be sure to keep to the time limit.

1 Choose a Team Coordinator.
2 Choose a Team Secretary (to take notes at meetings, keep everyone informed and keep people to deadlines).
3 AOB: Someone brings up this problem:

One manager has made an excuse not to be present today. You think he may be reluctant to come to team meetings because he has a much lower level of English than the rest of you. He told one of you that he doesn't feel he can contribute much. How can you encourage him to take part in future meetings?

Analysis
5 minutes

Did your team reach agreement on the three points within the time limit?
How did you choose the roles of Coordinator and Secretary?
Was it a natural choice or a difficult one?
In your discussions, who …
- reminded others about the goals of the meeting?
- kept an eye on the time?
- made the most creative suggestions?
- paid most attention to different people's opinions?
- offered to do something practical?

What do you think?
Whole group
15 minutes

Team roles

1 In any team, different people play different roles. That means they each behave, contribute and relate to others in a different way, depending on their personality. Is it a good thing that people play different roles within a team? Why? / Why not?

2 Match each of the main roles 1–3 with the types of behaviour a–h. There are two or more types of behaviour for each role.

1 Action role
2 People role
3 Ideas role

a Ask other people what they think or feel.
b Offer to do something practical.
c Remind people about goals.
d Put forward new suggestions.
e Try to reach a decision that everyone can agree with.
f Suggest an alternative viewpoint.
g Push people to make a decision.
h Delegate actions to people.

3 Which two roles do you think are most important for a good team coordinator to be able to play?

Good business practice, page 78

What do you say?
5 minutes

Playing a role in team meetings

Match the phrases below with the types of behaviour a–h above.

1 Remember that our main objective is ... (to save money).
2 Harry – could you take notes, please?
3 Maybe there's another way to look at this. We could ... (ask for more time).
4 Pete – you're looking worried. What are your thoughts on this?
5 I'll research the options and let you know next week.
6 Have you thought of ... (asking the customers)?
7 OK. We've discussed this point long enough. Can we try to come to an agreement?
8 Sarah, would this decision cause problems for you?

Grammar reference: Modal forms, page 86

Practice
Pairs
5 minutes

Choose one of these four roles: coordinator, team-worker, action role, ideas role. Think of what you might say in each of the situations below.

1 Someone wants to introduce a new agenda point which he/she feels strongly about. It would take a long time to discuss this point and it isn't very relevant to the goals of the meeting.
2 Four out of five team members agree to change a work routine. The fifth person is very unhappy about it.
3 Someone handed out a long discussion document at the start of a meeting. No one has had time to read it. It is important for the next agenda point.
4 The meeting should have finished half an hour ago. You still haven't decided on a key issue.

CD 6 Listening
15 minutes

The production team at Taylors Ltd, a clothing manufacturer, meets to discuss how they might handle an unusually large order which overstretches their capacity. These are the members of the team, in order of speaking:

Colin: Production Director and Team Coordinator
Lizzie: Manager, responsible for production schedules
Tim: Responsible for communication with other departments
Neil: A production supervisor, in charge of one of the production lines
Trisha: Quality Control Manager

1 Listen and answer the questions.

1 What two solutions to the problem are given at the start?
2 Why is Neil unhappy about the second solution?
3 What two reasons does Trisha give for objecting to the first solution?
4 What third suggestion is made? Could it work?
5 What is Tim going to do?

2 Listen again and say what language the team members use to do the following.

1 Summarise the problem and two possible solutions.
2 Bring Lizzie into the discussion.
3 Introduce another idea.
4 Delegate action to Tim.
5 End on a positive note.

Culture at work

Team-working

Attitudes towards teams and team-working may vary considerably in different companies and cultures. In collectivist cultures, team-working has been the norm for many years. The practice has now become more common in individualist cultures, too, though the nature of the team may differ. To what extent do you agree / disagree with the statements below? Complete your culture profile on page 82.

	Individualist	Collectivist
Goals	A team is a group of individuals who cooperate in order to serve their own interests: to win personal credit and success.	A team is a group of people who work together to achieve shared goals: success and credit for the group as a whole.
Information	Information is power. It may be in your best interests to keep some knowledge to yourself, or to share it with only one or two other people.	It is important to share all information with other members of your team. You should use your knowledge to help and support others.
Decision-making	The process of decision-making should be short in order to save time. If everyone doesn't agree, you could either vote or let a senior person make the decision.	It is important to reach consensus even if the decision-making process is slow. If some people don't agree, the team should take time to find the basis for agreement.

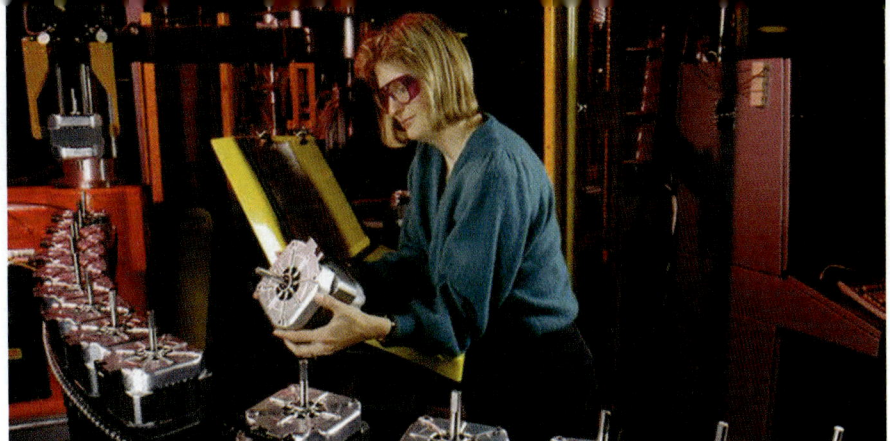

Task 2
Groups of 4–6
15–20 minutes

Objective: Play an active role

Read the case below and choose a role for yourself. (Note that there is now an extra role compared with *Practice* on page 15: troubleshooter.) Don't tell the others your role. Use it to help the team reach the best decision. If you see that someone else is playing the same role as you, or that there is no one fulfilling a key role, you may decide to change your role to balance the team.

Case

You are members of a team of six which is responsible for setting up a new production line at an engineering plant. You are all working overtime in order to complete the project by the end of the month. Now one of the key engineers in your team has been injured in an accident and will be off work for the next two weeks at least. Should you:

- try to manage with the remaining team members?
- bring in a new engineer to take the place of your colleague?
- try to persuade management to extend the deadline for the project?
- look for another solution?

Roles

A Coordinator: Remind the team of your main objectives; be positive and motivate people.
B Team-worker: Find out what others are thinking; try to find a solution that everyone can agree with.
C Action role 1: Offer to do something practical.
D Ideas role: Try to think of alternative ways of looking at the problem.
E Action role 2: Push the others to reach a decision quickly and efficiently.
F Troubleshooter: Point out the disadvantages of each idea.

Analysis
5 minutes

Did you recognise the roles the other team members played?
Did people play their roles successfully, do you think?
How easy did you find it to play your role?
Which kind of role do you feel most comfortable with?

Self-assessment

Think about your performance on the tasks. Were you able to:

- make a contribution? ☐ yes ☐ need more practice
- play an active role? ☐ yes ☐ need more practice

Unit 3 ■ 17

Writing 1 | Emails

| Make a strong start | Be friendly and diplomatic |

What do you write? 1 As businesspeople often receive a huge number of emails, it is important to ensure that yours will be noticed and read. Look at the strategies 1–5 for getting the attention of the reader and match them with the parts a–e of the email below.

1 Emphasise key information or any action that is required (for example, if you need a response by a certain date).
2 Include a relevant subject line to clarify the purpose of the email.
3 Provide any necessary context or background information that the reader will need.
4 Open with an appropriate salutation (*Hi ...* or *Hello ...* for people that you know and *Dear ...* for someone you are contacting for the first time).
5 When consolidating contact, refer to *when* and *where* you met the person.

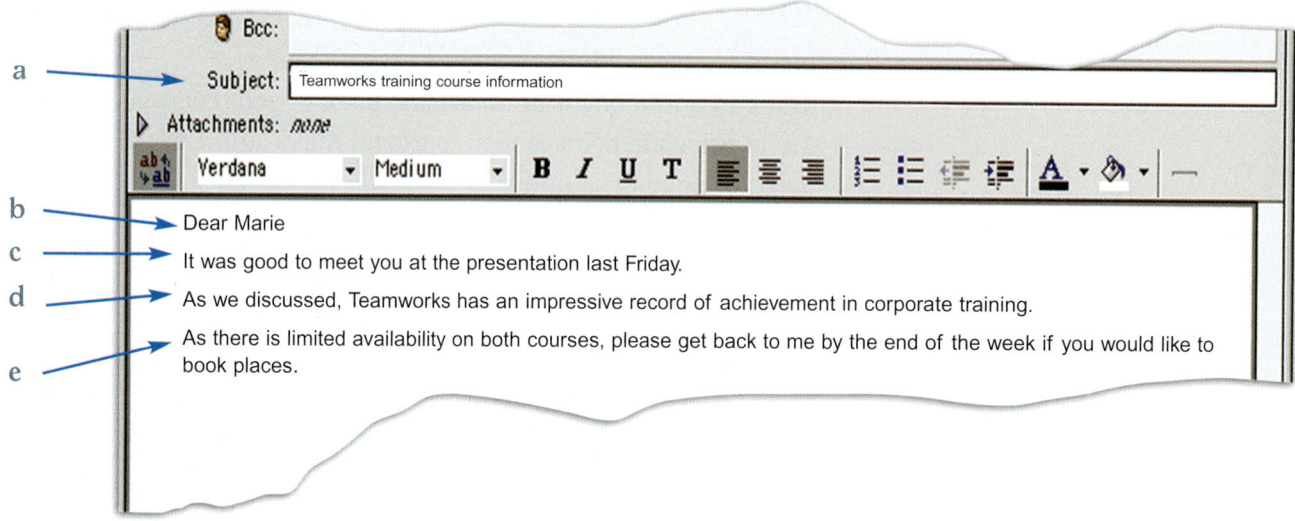

a — Subject: Teamworks training course information

b — Dear Marie

c — It was good to meet you at the presentation last Friday.

d — As we discussed, Teamworks has an impressive record of achievement in corporate training.

e — As there is limited availability on both courses, please get back to me by the end of the week if you would like to book places.

Task 1

Objective: Make a strong start

You work in the sales department of nTAG. Write an email to Mark Curtis, who you met for the first time at a conference last week. He would like to know what information can be included on the badges and what the advantages are for conference organisers and delegates. You are in his area on Friday; offer to visit his office and give a more detailed demonstration of the badge. (For more information on nTAG, look again at Unit 1.)

What do you think? Many people now work in 'virtual teams', which means that all, or almost all, of their communication is via email. It is still important to build a good relationship with other team members even if you never meet them.

A US company is working with a Japanese distributor to launch a new model (the Titan) in Japan. The US export manager replies to Yoshio Kurimoto about the launch schedule. Look at his email message below. Do you think the tone of it will help to build good team spirit? Why? / Why not?

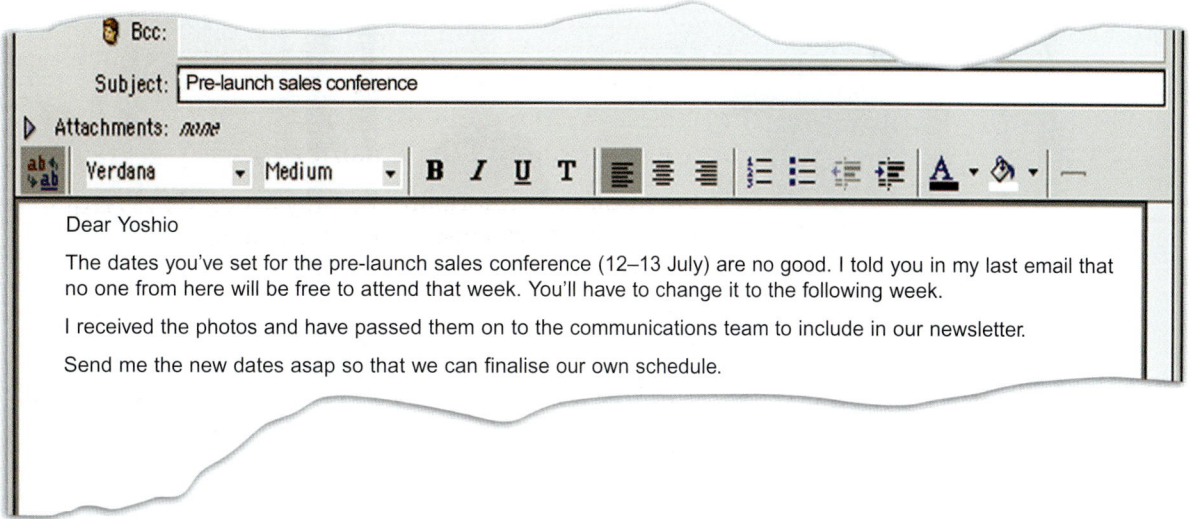

Dear Yoshio

The dates you've set for the pre-launch sales conference (12–13 July) are no good. I told you in my last email that no one from here will be free to attend that week. You'll have to change it to the following week.

I received the photos and have passed them on to the communications team to include in our newsletter.

Send me the new dates asap so that we can finalise our own schedule.

What do you write? 2 Look at the suggestions 1–4 for making your emails to colleagues more friendly and diplomatic. Match them with the phrases a–h.

1 Make requests polite and show consideration for people's workload

2 Show appreciation for other people's help or good work

3 Be fair and constructive if you need to criticise or point out errors

4 Include some friendly conversation and end with friendly greetings or good wishes

a This is just to remind you that we need to have your notes by the 13th so that we can ...

b Have a good trip next week!

c I'm afraid there seems to be a discrepancy / misunderstanding / slight problem ...

d Many thanks for sending ...

e Thanks very much for all your hard work on this.

f I realise you are very busy at present, but could you ... ?

g I really like your ideas – they're great!

h I won't be at my desk next week as I'm off to the sales conference in Jakarta – should be fun!

 Grammar reference: Modal forms, page 86

Task 2

Objective: Be friendly and diplomatic

Use appropriate phrases to expand the email in *What do you think?* into an email that is friendly and diplomatic. Refer to the launch schedule. Show consideration for the fact that changing the date will affect other scheduled events, too. Wish Yoshio success with the ad campaign.

Writing 1 ■ 19

Unit 4 — Ask questions

| Prepare questions | Ask for factual information | Find out about needs and interests |

Task 1
Whole group, divided in two
10 minutes

Objective: Prepare questions

Your company wants to set up a training programme in database analysis for staff. You are the company training manager and you have to identify an organisation that can run a customised training programme at your head office. Read about one of the prospective suppliers below, discuss what further information you need about the company and make a list of questions to ask.

Group A read about Headlamp Inc.
Group B read about Infos.

HEADLAMP INC
About us | The company | Locations
Consulting | Education | Research | Publications

Our experts

An Huang Dok   Dede Smith

INFOS
About us | What we do | Consulting services | Training | Newsletter

If your company is engaged in direct marketing, your customer database is your greatest asset. We can help you to exploit this asset by maximising your knowledge about existing customers (buying habits, perceptions, attitudes, motivation, future purchasing intentions) as well as prospective customers.

Database analysis means using every tool available to maximise the profit potential of marketing databases. We are an independent consulting firm specialised in database analysis, consulting and training.

| What do you say? | **Questioning a prospective supplier** |
| 5 minutes | |

Look at the questions and sentences a–g below which can all be used in an initial meeting with a prospective supplier. Which ones are useful for ...

1 organising a series of questions?
2 asking for sensitive information and being polite?
3 summarising or confirming what you already know?

a Can I start by asking some general questions about your company?
b Could you tell me how long you have been in this business?
c Your head office is in Chicago, isn't it?
d Could I ask how many people you employ?
e OK, let's move on to your training seminars ...
f So you could offer us customised training, is that right?
g Do you mind if I ask which other companies you have supplied?

 Grammar reference: Question forms, page 87

| Task 2 | **Objective: Ask for factual information** |
| Pairs (one person from each group; groups as in Task 1) | You are going to role-play two meetings between a training manager and a supplier. The training manager asks questions to find out about the supplier. Note down the answers and be ready to summarise the information at the end to check that it is correct. |

| Individually | **Before each meeting** |
| 5 minutes | |

Training manager:
    Organise the questions you prepared in Task 1 according to topic.
    Prepare a general question or statement to introduce each topic.
    Think about polite forms.

Supplier:
    Study your role brief and be ready to answer questions.

| Pairs | **Meeting 1** |
| 10 minutes | |

The training manager (buyer) meets a representative from Headlamp Inc.
Students from Group A: You are the training manager.
Students from Group B: Answer questions on Headlamp Inc.: turn to page 98.

| Pairs | **Meeting 2** |
| 10 minutes | |

The training manager (buyer) meets a representative from Infos.
Students from Group B: You are the training manager.
Students from Group A: Answer questions on Infos: turn to page 97.

Analysis	Did the training managers note down the correct information?
5 minutes	Did they organise their questions well?
	Did they ask questions politely or did it feel like an interrogation?
	Was there anything they didn't ask about?

What do you think?	**Questioning a prospective client**
Whole group	
5 minutes	

You are a supplier meeting a prospective client for the first time. Before making any offers, you have to find out about the buyer's needs and interests. Discuss the following questions.

1 Should you spend more time listening or talking?
2 How important is it to check the information you already have?
3 Is it better to ask too few or too many questions?
4 What kind of questions are most useful?

 Good business practice, page 78

What do you say?	**Asking about needs and interests**
5 minutes	

Look at questions a–d below. Which one ...

1 asks about priorities?
2 gets more information?
3 checks to see if you have the correct information?
4 is hypothetical?

a You want to train about 50 people, is that right?
b What else would you like to have?
c If we included follow-up training in the package, would that be of interest to you?
d What is more important for you: high quality or low cost?

Listening	Ronald Wheeler represents Lockstock, a company that provides data security software and consulting services. He has a meeting with Edwina West, a manager in a financial services company. Edwina's company may be interested in Lockstock's services.
15 minutes	

CD 7 **1** Listen to the first extract and answer the questions.

1 In which order does Ronald mention the following?
 a information systems b encryption software
 c current security arrangements
2 Is Ronald polite? If yes, what makes you think so?

CD 8 **2** Listen to the second extract and answer the questions.

1 What sensitive question does Ronald ask?
2 What hypothetical question does he ask?

CD 9 **3** Listen to the third extract and answer the questions.

1 How does Ronald find out about Edwina's interest in staff training?
2 What kind of question does he ask to find out about staff training?
 a a direct question b a hypothetical question c a check question

Culture at work

Questioning styles

In some cultures, people say exactly what they mean and it doesn't cause offence to ask direct questions. Other cultures prefer to talk in vaguer terms. They usually ask more general questions to avoid embarrassment. Which culture do you belong to? Complete your culture profile on page 82.

People from direct cultures ...	People from indirect cultures ...
use direct question forms and a decisive tone of voice to get the information they need.	use more polite questions (e.g. *Do you mind if I ask ... ?*) and a more gentle tone of voice.
ask closed questions to get specific information.	prefer to ask open questions that allow the other person to give as much information as they want.
see indirect cultures as vague and untrustworthy.	see direct cultures as hard and insensitive.

Task 3

Pairs (as in Task 2)
20 minutes
(5 minutes preparation + 5 minutes per meeting)

Objective: Find out about needs and interests

You are going to role-play another meeting between a buyer and supplier. In this meeting, the supplier will ask questions to find out about the buyer's needs.

The buyer is Elegante, a retailer selling women's fashions via the internet and direct mail. This company is interested in holding a training programme in database analysis for their staff.

Meeting 1

A representative from Headlamp Inc. meets with the training manager at Elegante. The meeting takes place at Elegante's offices in Paris.

Students from Group A: You are the training manager: turn to page 102.
Students from Group B: You represent Headlamp Inc.: turn to page 100.

Meeting 2

This time, a representative from Infos meets with the training manager at Elegante, again at Elegante's offices.

Students from Group A: You represent Infos: turn to page 100.
Students from Group B: You are the training manager: turn to page 102.

Analysis
5 minutes

Did the suppliers get all the available information about the client's needs?
Did they ask about priorities?
Did they check their facts?
Did they use hypothetical questions?

Self-assessment

Think about your performance on the tasks. Were you able to:

- prepare questions? ☐ yes ☐ need more practice
- ask for factual information? ☐ yes ☐ need more practice
- find out about needs and interests? ☐ yes ☐ need more practice

Unit 5 Present facts and figures

| Present figures accurately | Analyse information |

CD 10 Listening 1
5–10 minutes

Kenrig is an electrical goods retailer selling a range of household appliances including fridges, radios and mobile phones. Their mobile phone sales have increased rapidly in recent years.

Listen to the CEO briefing a team of researchers and note down two things that he asks them to do.

Task 1

Objective: Present figures accurately

Individually
10 minutes

Step 1 Preparation

Look at the information below and prepare a short presentation for the CEO of Kenrig. Do not try to present all the data: focus on the figures that you think are most important. Prepare visuals to highlight key information (use any material available, for example: paper, a flip chart, a white board).

Mobile phone subscribers in Africa		Mobile phone use
Mobile subscribers per 100 people (top 7 countries)		Number of mobile phone users (trans Africa) 60,000,000
South Africa	35	Growth 1998–2003 5,000%
Botswana	30	Mobile phones outnumber fixed lines 2:1
Morocco	23	(6% of Africans use mobile phones; 2.8% have fixed lines)
Gabon	20	Notes
Tunisia	12	South Africa: 85% of small businesses rely on mobile phones for business telecommunications.
Egypt	10	Egypt: 59% of businesses said mobile phone use was linked to an increase in profits.
Tanzania	5	Tanzania: 97% can access a mobile phone, 28% have access to a fixed line.
		Population (trans Africa 2005): 900,000,000

Pairs
5 minutes

Step 2 Presentation

Present the findings of your research to your partner.

The following language may be useful when presenting visuals.

Let's look at this diagram to get a better picture of ...
As this chart shows ...
If you look here ...
As you can see ...

When you present data, large figures are often rounded up or down, for example:

486%   ▲ *Just under / Nearly 500%*
2,535,030 ▼ *About / Around two and a half million*

Analysis
5 minutes

How did you decide which figures to focus on?
What information did you choose to present using visuals?
Were there any differences in the way that you and your partner interpreted the figures?
Did you both recommend the same countries to open the first outlets in?

What do you think?
Whole group
10 minutes

Presenting data

It is possible to change the impact or focus by presenting information in different ways, for example:

- by using phrases that imply an opinion.
   Only 2,000 customers responded. (negative)
   As many as 2,000 customers responded. (positive)
- by choosing a particular statistic to focus on.
   Almost 75% of Swedes are now connected to the internet.
   Over 25% of Swedes are still not connected to the internet.

Look at these extracts from a business technology magazine. In what other ways could these figures be expressed? What changes could the writer make to present the information in a more positive or more negative way?

1
The survey revealed that one in five mobile phone users did not know how to send text messages.

2
A spokesman for the company apologised to customers and said that, usually, the technical support team is able to deal with two-thirds of all problems within three hours.

3
Two cameras that incorporate the latest digital technology are the Pentram and the Omnex. Latest figures show that the Pentram is outselling the Omnex by two to one.

➔ Good business practice, page 77

Culture at work

How much detail?

When we are involved in cross-cultural presentations, it is useful to consider whether the audience is from a culture that is high context (does not require a lot of detail) or low context (requires a lot of detail). How much detail do you like to include in presentations? Complete your culture profile on page 82.

High context	Low context
Communication is often fast and economic.	Communication is often detailed. The presenting style will be explicit.
The presenter assumes that the audience will understand the facts or figures being discussed, so does not go into detailed explanation.	The presenter does not assume that the audience will understand the facts, so goes into detailed explanation.
Relies a lot on **non-verbal** communication (gestures, facial expressions) to read situations.	Relies on clear **verbal** or **visual** communication to read situations – data shown on visuals is likely to be supported by a verbal explanation.
Meaning is determined by **how** things are said, rather than by **what** is said.	Meaning is determined by **what** is said, rather than by **how** it is said.

CD 11 · Listening 2
10 minutes

Forseti Communications is an internet service provider (ISP). The company is exploring the possibility of entering the Asian internet market.

1 Listen to Sandra Andrews making an informal presentation about internet use in Mongolia. Are the following statements true or false? Correct any information that is wrong.

1. In 2005, there were 142,000 internet users in Mongolia.
2. The population of Mongolia in 2005 was around 2 1/2 million.
3. The number of internet users has grown by just over 500% between 2000 and 2005.
4. Approximately 5% of the population is over 65.
5. In 2015 the population will be about 4,000,000.

2 Say the correct version of all the numbers in the exercise. Listen again to check.

What do you say? 10 minutes	**Describing and interpreting figures**

Look at the phrases a–h from Sandra Andrews' presentation. Which can be used to ...

1 describe figures?
2 interpret data?

a this data suggests ...
b just over ...
c this represents a growth of ...
d these figures indicate that ...
e as much as ...
f this is significant because ...
g around ...
h this means that ...

 Grammar reference: Linking ideas 1, Relative clauses, page 89

Task 2	**Objective: Analyse information**

Individually 10 minutes	**Step 1 Preparation**

The project manager at Forseti Communications asks you to prepare a presentation on one of the two additional countries that are being considered as possible internet markets. Analyse the information you are given and prepare a two to three-minute presentation. You can create visuals to highlight key information or figures.

You can use the following language to help you move from point to point.

OK, I'll start by ...   Let's move on to ...
First ...   To sum up ...
Next ...

Student A turn to page 99.
Student B turn to page 100.

Groups of 4 10–15 minutes	**Step 2**

Make your presentation to the others. When you are listening, note down any key figures and information.

Analysis 5 minutes	How did you decide what information to focus on? How did you structure the information? What were the similarities and differences between presentations on the same countries?

Self-assessment	Think about how you performed on the tasks. Were you able to:
	– present figures accurately? ☐ yes ☐ need more practice
	– analyse information? ☐ yes ☐ need more practice

Unit 5 ■ 27

Unit 6 — Entertain guests

| Guide a conversation | Tell a story |

What do you think?
Pairs
10 minutes

What makes a good host?

How does a good host make guests feel comfortable and relaxed in your country? Write a list of things that a host should and shouldn't do. Discuss your ideas with a partner.

 Good business practice, page 76

What do you say?
10 minutes

Making conversation

1 Which of the underlined words or phrases in the conversation extracts 1–6 below could be replaced by one of the following words or phrases a–f?

a so
b well
c I don't really know
d actually
e incidentally
f mind you

1 I visited the new company headquarters last week. It's a lovely building. <u>Still</u>, I'm not sure I'd want to work there: it's a bit modern for me.
2 Yes, we had a great time in Hong Kong. <u>By the way</u>, thanks for recommending that restaurant in Kowloon: it was excellent.
3 Why didn't he get the promotion? <u>I'm not really sure</u>.
4 ... and the food was dreadful, too. <u>Anyway</u>, as I was saying, we had just arrived at the hotel when there was a knock on the door ...
5 No, I haven't been to the top of the KL Tower. <u>To be honest</u>, I'm not very good with heights.
6 ... and when it was time to pay, I suddenly realised that I didn't have my wallet with me. It was, <u>you know</u>, really embarrassing.

28 ■ Unit 6

2 Match two of the twelve words and phrases from exercise 1 with each of the following functions.

1. Change the direction of the conversation
2. Go back to the previous topic of conversation
3. Pause or gain time to think
4. Politely contradict what has just been said
5. Avoid commenting
6. Being sincere, saying something is true

Practice
5–10 minutes

Complete these sentences using one of the words or phrases from *What do you say?* exercise 1. More than one answer is possible for each sentence. Use each word or phrase only once.

1. This is a lovely restaurant. _____, as we were saying about your new job …
2. It was the worst place imaginable to entertain clients. _____, I had a good time!
3. Oh, you think he's a bad manager, do you? _____.
4. _____ I don't really like nightclubs; I'd prefer to go somewhere quieter.
5. So then I spent an hour wandering around Tallin, which is a beautiful city _____, and I still couldn't remember where I'd parked the car …
6. You'd like to discuss the plans now? _____, it might be better to wait until we get back to the office. I have all the details there.

Task 1

Objective: Guide a conversation

Groups of 4
5 minutes

Step 1 Brainstorm

Hold a three-minute meeting to brainstorm conversation topics that would be suitable to talk about with a business contact who you do not know well (weather, holidays, etc.). Then make a note of the topics that you think are most useful.

Pairs
10 minutes

Step 2 Make conversation

You work for the Amerti advertising agency. You have been asked to look after an important guest at a company party. Take turns to be the host and the guest. Read your information card and have a short conversation. Try to avoid any long silences. When you have finished the conversation, change roles.

Host turn to page 97.
Guest turn to page 98.

Analysis
5 minutes

As the host, were you able to keep the conversation going?
What did you do if the guest seemed uninterested in the topic that you introduced?
When you were the guest, did you contribute to the conversation?

Unit 6 ■ 29

CD 12 Listening
15 minutes

1 Luke Marlow is at the Amerti party. Listen to him telling his guest, Donna Bertoli, a story. Answer the questions and then put the information in the order that you hear it in the story.

1 Who is the story about?
2 Where does the story take place?
3 Why were people angry?
4 When does the story take place?
5 What did the man throw in the pool?

2 Listen again. Who says the following, Luke or Donna?

a Right.
b It turned out ...
c Guess what ...
d Really?
e You've got to hear this ...
f Why was that?
g Go on ...
h Apparently ...

3 Use your answers to exercise 1, and some of the phrases from exercise 2, to practise retelling the story to your partner. Were there any differences between your account and your partner's?

What do you say?
5 minutes

Telling and responding to a story

When we tell a story, it helps to use phrases that build the listener's anticipation and gain interest. In some cultures, the storyteller may think that the listener is bored if he or she does not regularly express interest. Match the functions 1–8 below with the expressions a–h from Listening exercise 2.

Telling a story

1 Gain interest at the start of a story
2 Get the audience to anticipate
3 Introduce information you are not 100% sure is true
4 Talk about the outcome

Listening to a story

5 Say you want the story to continue
6 Ask questions
7 Show you are paying attention
8 Show interest or surprise

Culture at work

Ways of telling a story

Some cultures tell stories in a linear way, and focus on a single topic or a few closely related topics. Other cultures use a more circular style of storytelling where a number of different topics are developed at the same time. When you tell a story, are you more topic-centred or topic-associating? Complete your culture profile on page 82.

Topic-centred	Topic-associating
Focus is on a single topic or a small number of topics that are closely linked.	Includes a number of loosely related topics. The link between topics may not seem immediately obvious.
Events are generally described in the order in which they happened.	Events are not necessarily described in the order in which they happened.
The speaker provides background information to help the listener understand the story.	The speaker assumes shared knowledge so does not provide background information.

Task 2

Objective: Tell a story

Pairs
10 minutes

Step 1 Preparation

Prepare a story that you would feel comfortable telling to a business acquaintance. Use any story you know such as a personal experience or, for example, the story of a book, film or advert, or something from the news. Discuss your stories and help each other to prepare them.

Different pairs
10 minutes

Step 2 Tell the story

Change partners and take turns to tell your story. When you are listening to your partner's story, show that you are interested.

Analysis
5 minutes

How did you structure your story?
What phrases did you use to make it interesting?
When you were the listener, how did you show that you were interested?

 Grammar reference: Review of tenses 2, page 84

Self-assessment

Think about your performance on the tasks. Were you able to:
- guide a conversation?   ☐ yes   ☐ need more practice
- tell a story?   ☐ yes   ☐ need more practice

Writing 2 | Factual reports

Write an executive summary

What do you think?

1 What factors can make a report easy or difficult to read? Think about the last report that you read.

- Did it have a clear, logical structure?
- Was it easy to follow?

2 Look at the items 1–6. Which part a–c of a report would you expect to find them in?

1 Main arguments, findings and evidence
2 Summary of the main conclusions
3 Recommendations for action
4 Appendices (section for supplementary information)
5 Graphs, tables, charts to illustrate key facts
6 Purpose of the report

a The opening paragraphs
b The body of the report
c The end of the report

What do you write? 1 It is a good idea to use visual clues to guide the reader and to structure paragraphs. Look at the report extract below and match the parts with the following.

1 (Numbered) subheading   2 Bullet point   3 (Numbered) heading
4 Bold typeface   5 List

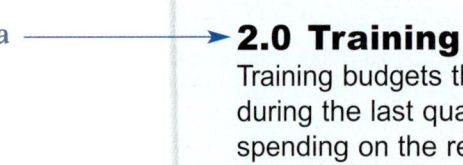

a → **2.0 Training**
Training budgets throughout the company were re-evaluated during the last quarter, allowing department heads to focus spending on the requirements of their staff. After consulting with departmental managers, it was agreed that seminars would be held on:

b →
• database analysis
• spreadsheets
c → • effective use of Powerpoint presentations.

d → **2.1 Database analysis seminar**
The department intends to offer one full-day training seminar in this area, although further courses may be scheduled if required. Two main training organisations were considered for the seminar: **Infos** and **Headlamp Inc**. After analysing course content, it was decided that ...

e

What do you write? 2 An **executive summary** is sometimes circulated independently of the main report. It gives the gist of the main information and means it isn't necessary to read the entire document. An executive summary usually contains:

- the purpose of the report
- any necessary recommendations
- conclusions.

1 Match the functions 1–4 with the words and phrases a–l that you can use when writing an executive summary.

1 Introduce conclusions or recommendations
2 Give ideas that show a contrast
3 Add a point or idea
4 Focus attention on a specific topic or idea

a	Regarding ...	e	While ...	i	Concerning ...
b	Furthermore ...	f	For this reason ...	j	Whereas ...
c	However ...	g	Consequently ...	k	As a result ...
d	Therefore ...	h	Nevertheless ...	l	In addition ...

2 Look at this extract from an executive summary and underline the correct word in *italics*.

Executive summary

Introduction
The aim of the report is to explain why sales of the Demarco CX Printer failed to reach expected targets. The product launch initially produced encouraging results in the domestic market, ¹*whereas / regarding* the overseas market was a little slower to respond ...

Conclusions
Market research carried out at the R&D stage suggested that this market was oversubscribed. ²*Furthermore / Nevertheless*, we believed that the unique selling points of the CX would lead to success in this market without the need for any increase in the marketing budget. ³*Therefore / While* other, lower-priced brands were able to retain their market share, the cost of the CX proved ...

Recommendations
There are two main recommendations for improving sales of the CX.
⁴*Concerning / In addition to* advertising, a new advertising campaign will be needed to highlight the unique selling points. ⁵*Regarding / Consequently*, the marketing budget will need to be increased by approximately 15% ...

Task

Objective: Write an executive summary

You have written a detailed report on one of the following topics. Write the executive summary (maximum one page) for the report.

- A project that you are / have recently been involved with
- A training course that you have attended
- Main challenges for your country / company in the next five years

 Grammar reference: Linking ideas 2, page 90

Unit 7 Bid and bargain

| Make proposals and counter-proposals | Bargain for agreement |

Task 1
Pairs
20 minutes

Objective: Make proposals and counter-proposals

Medea is a well-known pop star who recently hit the headline news when it became known that she was 'very friendly' with a royal prince. The relationship has now ended, but she wants to publish a book telling her story. Her agent is in negotiation with a publisher to sign a contract for the book. You are going to play the roles of Medea's agent and the publisher's representative and try to reach agreement about the advance.

You may want to use some of the following language.

What do you have in mind?
I'd like to propose ...
I think you can do better than that.
We have to take into consideration ...
In that case, we could ...
No way! That's out of the question!
That sounds fine. You've got a deal!

Student A: You are Medea's agent, turn to page 97.
Student B: You are the publisher's representative, turn to page 100.

Take a few minutes to prepare your role. Then hold a negotiation with your partner.

Analysis
10 minutes

What amount did you agree?
Compare your deal with other pairs – who got the best deal?
Who made the first proposal?
Was it accepted quickly?
What did you find out about the other person's position?

What do you think?
Whole group
5–10 minutes

Negotiating

What conclusions can you draw from the role-play above? Think about the following questions.

- Is it a good idea to set a target for what you want?
- Does making the first proposal put you at an advantage or a disadvantage?
- Does it help to discuss factors other than money? Why?
- Does it help to find out more about your partner's position? Why?

 Good business practice, page 78

What do you say?
5 minutes

Bidding and bargaining

Match the functions 1–7 with the phrases a–j below that you can use in a negotiation.

1 Stating needs
2 Responding positively
3 Responding negatively
4 Responding without commitment
5 Giving justification
6 Generating options
7 Bargaining (conditional offers)

a It's important for us to have 24-hour service because we work through the night.
b Here's another idea. We could put a penalty clause in the contract in case of delays.
c We'll increase our offer if you can guarantee delivery by the end of January.
d I see what you mean. But how would that work?
e We really need delivery by the 14th.
f We could agree to that if you paid us 50 per cent up front.
g We will have to raise our price if you insist on early delivery.
h I'm afraid that could be a problem.
i What if we included service in the price? Would that help?
j We have no problem with that.

 Grammar reference: Conditionals, page 95

CD 13 Listening
15 minutes

Heath Robinson & Sons are supplying Smelting Pot plc with an important piece of equipment for their manufacturing process, and the agreed implementation date is 1 March. The representatives of the two companies are now meeting to negotiate some of the details.

Listen to three extracts from the negotiation, in which the buyer and supplier discuss several points in the sales contract, and make notes. Then fill in the table.

	Supplier's proposal	Buyer's proposal	Counter-proposal
Delivery date			
Installation and testing			
Advance payment			
Penalty clause			

Culture at work

Bargaining

Approaches to bargaining and negotiating can vary according to whether a company or culture is deal-focused or relationship-focused. Most negotiators lie somewhere between the two extremes. It is useful not only to recognise where your counterpart in the negotiation is placed, but also to identify which style reflects your own attitude to bargaining. How would you describe your culture? Complete your culture profile on page 82.

	Deal-focused	Relationship-focused
Start the bargaining process	It is important to get down to business as quickly as possible.	It is important to develop a relationship before getting down to business.
Contracts	Written agreements are essential to prevent misunderstandings and to solve problems.	Personal trust is more important than a detailed contract.
Verbal communication	It is better to be direct so that you can be clearly understood.	Indirect language helps to maintain harmony. It is very important to avoid giving offence.
Sincerity	It is better to be honest and say if something can't be done.	If you can't do something, you can at least show willingness to try.

Task 2
Pairs

Objective: Bargain for agreement

The buyer, a representative of Smelting Pot plc, and the supplier, a representative of Heath Robinson & Sons, meet and discuss the following points in the sales contract for the new equipment: payment terms, period of warranty and after-sales service contract.

Payment terms: The supplier is asking for an advance payment of 40%.

Supplier's warranty – standard terms
- Covers manufacturer's faults: not accidents or wear and tear.
- Covers replacement of all faulty parts, free call-out and labour costs where repairs are carried out.
- Period of warranty is one year.

After-sales service contract
- The manufacturer's engineer can be called within normal working hours.
- Manufacturer guarantees to answer the call within one working day.
- 24-hour immediate call-out service costs an additional €3,000 per year.

---

5 minutes — **Step 1 Preparation**

Student A: You are a representative of Smelting Pot plc: turn to page 101.
Student B: You are a representative of Heath Robinson & Sons: turn to page 102.

Decide which points you want most and which points you could compromise on.

15 minutes — **Step 2 Negotiation**

Negotiate the best deal you can with your partner. Discuss each point before making definite offers or trying to reach agreement. Find out where your partner may be ready to compromise.

Analysis
10 minutes

Did you and your partner reach agreement? If not, why not?
On which points did you get what you wanted? Where did you compromise? (Compare your deal with other pairs.)
Did you find out as much as you could about your partner's position?
Did you keep your options open?

Self-assessment

Think about your performance on the tasks. Were you able to:

- make proposals and counter-proposals? ☐ yes ☐ need more practice
- bargain for agreement? ☐ yes ☐ need more practice

Unit 8 Chair a meeting

| Control a meeting | Deal with people effectively |

Task 1

Objective: Control a meeting

Groups of 4
10 minutes

Step 1 Discussion

Have a short meeting to discuss the main duties and responsibilities of a chairperson. You are all equally responsible for making sure that:

- everyone has a chance to put forward their views
- no individual dominates
- everyone keeps to the point
- notes are taken.

Whole group
5 minutes

Step 2 Feedback

Present your group's ideas to the other groups.

Analysis
5 minutes

What were the advantages and disadvantages of not having a chairperson in your meeting?
Did everyone have a chance to put forward their ideas?
What tactics did you use to stop any individuals dominating?
Did your group manage to keep to the point?
How did you decide who would take notes?

What do you think?
Pairs
10 minutes

Different types of behaviour

Look at the following examples of behaviour that a chairperson might have to deal with in a meeting. Which situation(s) should the chairperson deal with most urgently? Compare your ideas with your partner. Discuss what strategies the chairperson could use in each situation.

- A participant looks bored and is not contributing to the discussion.
- Every time anyone makes a suggestion, one participant responds with a negative comment. They say why an idea won't work, but don't make any positive suggestions.
- Two participants keep having private, whispered discussions during the meeting.
- A participant doesn't want to listen to anyone else's ideas. They keep interrupting and try to dominate any topic discussed.
- A participant is not very willing to give an opinion.
- A participant keeps introducing irrelevant topics to the discussion.

Good business practice, page 79

Grammar reference: Adjectives and adverbs, page 93

Culture at work

The function of a chairperson

In some cultures the main role of the chairperson is to control the meeting. This may include sticking to an agenda, keeping order and making sure that the meeting does not overrun. In other cultures the function of the chairperson might be to encourage participation and agreement. What is the main function of a chairperson in meetings in your country? Complete your culture profile on page 82.

Consensus-oriented	Results-oriented
In difficult situations, the chairperson may focus on compromise and mediation.	In difficult situations, the chairperson may attempt to control the meeting and use formal rules to keep order.
The chairperson may define their role as that of helping to achieve agreement or consensus.	The chairperson may define their role as that of helping to achieve objectives or decide on a series of action points.

CD 14 Listening
10–15 minutes

1 Listen to extracts from four meetings. Match the meetings 1–4 to the behaviours a–d.

a Try to introduce irrelevant topics
b Respond negatively to other people's ideas
c Try to dominate
d Do not respond initially

2 Match each of the situations 1–4 with two of the phrases a–h that the chairperson uses to deal with them. Listen again and check your answers.

Situation

Participant(s) ...
1 try to dominate.
2 do not respond.
3 respond negatively.
4 try to introduce irrelevant topics.

Chairperson

a We need consensus.
b You obviously feel strongly about this.
c If nobody has any better ideas, how about ... ?
d It is important we keep to the point on this.
e I'd like to hear what other people think.
f So, how do you think we should approach this?
g We've got a lot to get through and time is running out.
h Thank you for your comments. We'll take them into consideration.

What do you say?
10 minutes

Dealing with difficult people

Look at the suggestions below for dealing with difficult situations and choose the response that you think would work best.

1 Help calm a difficult situation by acknowledging how the person feels.
   a You're obviously pretty angry about this.
   b I can see that you feel strongly about this.
2 Try to find out why the person is being difficult.
   a Can you explain why you feel this way?
   b Why are you being unreasonable?
3 Show that you understand.
   a I can sympathise with your concerns.
   b I realise why you're panicking about this.
4 Encourage quiet participants when they contribute, even if you don't agree with their ideas.
   a Thanks for your suggestion, but you really need to think it through a bit more.
   b I think the basic idea is good, but perhaps we could discuss some of the details.
5 Be firm if people try to use the meeting to speak about personal grievances.
   a This isn't the best place to discuss this.
   b Leave your personal differences out of this.

Task 2
Groups of 4
40 minutes

Objective: Deal with people effectively

You are going to role-play four short meetings. For each meeting, read the situation and objective below and look at your information at the back of the book. You are the chairperson for one of the meetings and a participant for the other three.

When you are the chairperson, start the meeting by outlining the objective. During the meeting, try to make sure that everyone has a chance to participate and deal with any negative tactics that participants use.

Student A turn to page 99. Student C turn to page 102.
Student B turn to page 100. Student D turn to page 104.

Meeting 1
Situation
Your company manufactures a car which has always been popular with older consumers and families because the brand image is safe and reliable. For the last two years there has been a steady decline in market share.
Objective
Discuss whether to stay with your current consumers or create a new brand image to appeal to another segment of the market.

Meeting 2
Situation
Your company is sponsoring a new magazine aimed at businesspeople who are learning English. You are on the committee liaising with the publishers.
Objective
Think of five subjects for articles to suggest to the publisher for the first edition of the magazine.

Meeting 3
Situation
Your company manufactures camping and outdoor adventure equipment. A mistake by the purchasing department means that you now have a large quantity of waterproof material that is surplus to requirements. It is not possible to return the material to the supplier.
Objective
Brainstorm ways that you could put the material to use.

Meeting 4
Situation
Your company has invested a lot of money creating a brand identity for a new toothpaste. An employee has just discovered that the product name sounds like the word *toothache* in the language of one country where you plan to market the toothpaste.
Objective
Discuss possible ways to approach the problem.

Analysis
5 minutes

When you were the chairperson, what type of behaviour did you find most difficult to deal with?
What strategies did you use to encourage people to participate and to discourage negative tactics?
When you were a participant who was acting in a negative way, how did this affect the meeting?
Did the chairperson deal with your behaviour effectively?

Self-assessment

Think about your performance on the tasks. Were you able to:
- control a meeting? ☐ yes ☐ need more practice
- deal with people effectively? ☐ yes ☐ need more practice

Unit 9 Emphasise your point

| Emphasise priorities | Make your point strongly |

Task 1

Objective: Emphasise priorities

Pairs
10 minutes

Step 1 Preparation

Read the brief and the actions in the list below. With your partner, agree which **one** action you think is the most urgent. Work together to prepare a short argument lasting about one minute. Emphasise why you need to make this action your priority.

Brief

One of you is a scientist who has invented an exciting new product: a synthetic textile which you have trialled very successfully. Your partner is a business graduate with experience in the textile industry. You decide to set up your own business to manufacture and sell the new textile. However, you need to raise funding to start the business.

Actions

Work out how you could manufacture on a large scale.

Carry out market research.   Take out a patent.

Ask the bank for funding.   Prepare a business plan.

Other (your idea): _____

You may want to use some of the following language.

We really need to … / It's essential to …
This is absolutely imperative and should be at the top of the list …
Otherwise we can't …
We really ought to do this urgently because …

Groups of 3–4 5 minutes	**Step 2 Presentation** Present your argument to the others in the group.
Analysis 5 minutes	Who gave the most effective presentation? What do you think made their argument effective? Give reasons.
CD 15 Listening 1 5 minutes	**1** The two partners in the case above were Jimmy Whitecoat and Penny Ledger. Listen to first Jimmy and then Penny giving their view about what action they should take. What does each one say they should do first? **2** Which of them do you think emphasises the priorities more effectively? Give reasons.
What do you say? 5 minutes	**Emphasising your point** Look at the following ways of making your point more emphatic. 1 Using signals to focus attention on what you are about to say: *OK! This is the plan.* *This is what we have to do to achieve our goals.* 2 Using strong words: *Let's be **absolutely** clear about this!* *It's **essential** / **imperative** to …* 3 Using the full form instead of a contraction: *This is **not** what we want.* (instead of *isn't*) *We **will** succeed.* (instead of *we'll*) 4 Building sentences around key words which you stress when speaking: *What we want is more **security**.* *It's the **price** that's important.* *It isn't only the **cost** that's a problem: it's also the **time**.*
CD 16 Listening 2 5 minutes	Listen to Penny again. Which of the strategies 1–4 above does she use? Identify examples.
Practice 1 5 minutes	Make the following statements more emphatic and then practise saying them in an emphatic way. 1 Taking out a patent should be our first step. 2 We should get some advice. 3 Making a profit is important. 4 We need more time. 5 This isn't the best way to attract investment. 6 It's a difficult and risky market. 7 We have to find a new manager. 8 I think we'll have sufficient funds.

Grammar reference: Emphasis, page 88

Power talk

What do you think?
Whole group
5 minutes

What other factors make people sound more powerful when they talk? Discuss the effect of the following.

- Tone of voice
- Hesitation
- Tentative opinions
- Taking or denying responsibility (e.g. *I'm not really an expert on this*)
- Positive or negative language

Good business practice, page 80

CD 17 Listening 3
10 minutes

1 Another way to emphasise your point is to stress key words. Jimmy and Penny have a meeting with a venture capitalist, Max Cash, who tells them what they have to do to attract investors. Read the script of Max's argument below.

Underline the words you think Max will stress most. Mark any pauses within sentences using ||. (The first sentence has been marked as an example.)

OK. I've heard your proposal || and this is what I think. You have an excellent product here. It's something different, something special. And that's a huge point in your favour. But – and this is a big 'but' – can you sell this product and make a profit? It's the market for the product that's important and at the moment we simply don't know if there is a market out there. As an investor, what I want to know is: who are you planning to sell to? Why will these people want to buy your product? How many people will buy it? And what price will they pay? Market research should be your absolute priority now.

2 Now listen and see if you marked the stresses and pauses according to the way Max spoke.

Practice 2
Pairs
5 minutes

Work with a partner. Practise reading the text aloud using appropriate word stress and pauses.

Culture at work — **Showing emotion**

How much you show your emotions may depend on the culture you belong to. In affective cultures, people often express strong feelings when they give a point of view. In neutral cultures, people control their feelings. Which culture do you belong to? Complete your culture profile on page 82.

People in affective cultures ...	People in neutral cultures ...
use more emotive language: *I'm really excited! This is a great project!*	use moderate language: *I'm pleased to be involved in this project.*
often speak loudly, in an animated way and with a wide variety of tones.	often speak rather quietly, in a flat, inexpressive tone.
prefer presentations that are lively.	prefer presentations to be given calmly.
may think that people who don't show their feelings are disinterested.	may think that people who display too much feeling are 'out of control'.

Task 2 Objective: Make your point strongly

Individually — 10 minutes

Step 1 Preparation

Choose one of the situations below and prepare to present your argument. Alternatively, choose any situation from your own experience where you have had to argue strongly for a particular point of view. You will be arguing against the common point of view, so you will need to make your point strongly!

Situation 1

You belong to a group of investors. The other people in your group want to invest all the funds in well-established markets with high security. You think it would be better to invest 15 per cent of your funds in high-risk investments where you could get higher returns.

For points to include in your argument turn to page 99.

Situation 2

You and your business partners are setting up a new high-class restaurant. You want to employ Giorgio Fusilli, a top chef. However, he is demanding a 30 per cent share of the business, on top of a generous salary. Your partners would prefer to see Giorgio as an employee, not as a business partner, but you think you should give Giorgio the share he wants.

For points to include in your argument turn to page 100.

Whole group — 10 minutes

Step 2 Presentation

Each person should present their argument.

Analysis — 5 minutes

How far were you convinced by each person's argument?
Did they use appropriate signals to focus attention?
Did they make good use of emphatic language?
Did they use appropriate word stress and pauses to highlight the main ideas?

Self-assessment

Think about your performance on the tasks. Were you able to:
- emphasise priorities?   ☐ yes   ☐ need more practice
- make your point strongly?   ☐ yes   ☐ need more practice

Writing 3 | Memos

| Organise the information | Write a clear proposal |

What do you write? 1 It is common for people to receive memos that are not especially relevant to them. When writing a memo, therefore, it is important to start with a sentence that makes the purpose clear. Look at the following reasons for writing memos.

1 Give instructions or directives (e.g. to follow new policy / regulations)
2 Remind people about deadlines or dates
3 Respond to an enquiry
4 Give a summary of a trip or meeting

Match the reasons 1–4 above with the purpose statements a–d.

a This memo responds to your request to research ethical investment funds.
b This memo presents an overview of the visit to Jordan, 14–18 May.
c This is to inform you of changes in procedures for submitting budgets.
d Quarterly financial reports are due by 15 March.

What do you think? Memos need to be short and concise. New information should be highlighted at the top of the memo and not 'hidden' among unnecessary details. In what order would you put the following in a well-structured memo?

1 Supporting information: details, examples, further arguments
2 Key point(s): new information or instructions
3 Contact details: email / phone number of sender
4 Purpose of memo

Task 1

Objective: Organise the information

Reorganise the information in the memo below. It will help your readers to access the information more quickly if you can use bullet points for some of the information.

Memo

To: All Departmental Managers
From: Central Administration, Legal Department
Subject: New fire safety regulations

Managers should check that all fire-fighting equipment and alarm systems are of the approved standard and that instructions for using the equipment are clearly displayed. Please give this your urgent attention. You should also check that an emergency plan for evacuating the building is prepared and that maps showing nearest fire exits and escape routes are posted in each room. Queries to Phil Deacon, extension 928, or email phildeacon@ashleys.com. All managers are required to ensure that their department complies fully with the regulations. Following recent government legislation, new fire safety regulations come into force on 1 July.

What do you write? 2 If the purpose of your memo is to propose action (rather than give instructions or information), use the following plan.

1. Explain the current situation
2. Outline your proposal
3. Stress the benefits of following your proposal
4. Call for action

Put paragraphs a–d in the correct order to match the plan above.

a I therefore propose that we hold a meeting to review the schedule and set new deadlines. I suggest Wednesday 9 April at 10:00 for this meeting.

b The project is currently three weeks behind schedule and it is clear that we will be unable to meet the 1 May deadline. This is causing considerable stress among team members. In addition, our clients need to be given a reliable date for completion.

c Please confirm that you are able to attend this meeting. It is important that as many people as possible attend.

d Revising the schedule will reduce the pressure on staff and enable us to give our clients a more realistic completion date.

Grammar reference: Review of tenses 1, The passive, page 83

Task 2

Objective: Write a clear proposal

Step 1

Look at the notes below which a manager used to prepare a memo to propose reducing the frequency of meetings. Organise the points in the notes as suggested in *What do you write? 2*.

Step 2

Rewrite the notes to create a memo of four paragraphs.

Notes

- Change to monthly meetings – best solution: first Monday of each month – hold extra meetings if necessary
- Team members say: weekly meetings waste time – often not much to discuss – most info could be shared via email
- Consider this proposal – send comments by Friday
- Monthly meetings: focus on most important points only – more efficient – save time

Unit 10 | Manage a crisis

| Prepare an action plan | Hold a crisis meeting |

What do you think?
Pairs
5–10 minutes

Dealing with a crisis

Look at these ways of dealing with a crisis situation. Which things would you do to prepare for a crisis and which would you do during a crisis?

1. Brainstorm problems that might happen.
2. Carry out a risk assessment.
3. Identify what action is required most urgently.
4. Prepare an action plan for each potential crisis situation.
5. Make decisions calmly.
6. Discuss how to solve the problem.

What things could you do after the crisis has been dealt with to make sure that the same problems do not occur again?

Good business practice, page 81

Listening
10 minutes

The Condite group is planning a big summer party for employees and important clients. The project leader organising the event is chairing a meeting to assess risks. The participants have just finished brainstorming problems that might happen at the party.

CD 18

1 Listen and tick the potential problems they mention.

1 Catering ☐   5 Medical emergencies and accidents ☐
2 Bad weather ☐   6 Fire ☐
3 Transport ☐   7 Security ☐
4 Natural disasters ☐ 8 Room size ☐

48 ▪ Unit 10

CD 19 **2** Listen to the rest of the conversation, where they decide on an action plan for one of the potential problem areas. Look at the extract from their action plan and correct five mistakes.

Action plan: Medical emergencies and fire

Team coordinator: Ellen

Medical back-up
- Hotel medical facilities (all emergencies)
- 11 staff trained in first aid (minor accidents)

Miscellaneous
- Heat: Arrange 2 rooms where guests can rest
  Catering team to provide coffee
- Indoor swimming pool: 4 members of staff to watch the pool (rota)

Task 1
Groups of 4–6

10 minutes

Objective: Prepare an action plan

Step 1 Anticipate problems

You are helping to organise a conference. As part of the preparation, your team has been asked to anticipate what things could go wrong before and during the conference. Look at the conference details below and discuss all the problems that might occur. Identify the five that you think require an action plan.

Conference details

Conference title: The Future of Energy
Location: Hotel Primo, Lake Garda, Italy
Date: 12–14 January

Special guest speaker: Professor Edmund Martin, Science author and TV presenter

Additional presenters: 15 (3 Spanish, 2 Canadian, 1 American, 2 Japanese, 1 French, 2 German, 2 British, 2 Italian)

70% of the presentations will be multi-media

Expected attendance: approx 140 delegates

A welcome buffet and use of a shuttle bus to and from the airport and train stations are included in the conference ticket price, as well as entrance to all seminars and presentations.

Additional information:

- Professor Martin has asked for a ground floor suite or access via a lift as his recent operation makes the use of stairs difficult.
- The Lake Garda Music Festival will be taking place at the same time as the conference. Guests at the Energy conference can purchase tickets to hear Antonio Vivardi, the opera star, give a special performance at the Hotel Primo on 13 January.

10–15 minutes

Step 2 Make a plan

Prepare a short action plan to recommend how to deal with each of the five potential problems you identified.

You can use some of the following language.

What happens if ... ?
What can we do about ... ?
If ... happens, we could ...
As far as ... is concerned, we should ...

Analysis
5 minutes

Was your group able to agree on what to include in the action plans?
How did different group members approach the problems?

Grammar reference: Reference words, page 92

Grammar reference: Conditionals, page 95

Culture at work

Attitudes to risk

Different people approach problem solving in different ways, according to their attitude to risk. In cultures with high uncertainty avoidance, people prefer to avoid risk. In cultures with low uncertainty avoidance, people are more likely to take risks. What is the attitude to risk in your culture? Complete your culture profile on page 82.

High uncertainty avoidance	Low uncertainty avoidance
People prefer to avoid risk, so will have detailed plans in place, in case things go wrong.	People are more likely to react to circumstances than plan in advance.
People may feel threatened by uncertain or unknown situations and avoid circumstances which could cause uncertainty.	Unknown situations and change do not usually cause stress or anxiety.
Rules, regulations and controls are introduced to reduce the amount of uncertainty in situations.	Rules, regulations and controls are avoided and kept to a minimum: flexibility is preferred.

What do you say?
10 minutes

Find a solution

Match each of the functions 1–3 with two of the phrases a–f that you can use to talk about solutions.

1 Ask for ideas
2 Divide the problem into parts
3 Suggest ideas

a How can we sort this out?
b We'll just have to …
c The first thing we should do is …
d We need to …
e How do you suggest we deal with this?
f Let's just take it one step at a time.

Task 2
Groups of 4

Objective: Hold a crisis meeting

5 minutes

Step 1 Preparation

Prepare a crisis situation for another group to discuss. Imagine that a problem has occurred at the Energy conference. Write a short description giving details about what has happened. Give the notes to another group. Take the crisis situation that the other group has prepared for you.

15 minutes

Step 2 Meeting

Ask one of your group to read out the situation. Hold a crisis meeting to deal with the situation. All members of the group should look for solutions and make suggestions.

Analysis
5–10 minutes

How well did your group perform as a team during the crisis meeting? What could your group do to improve its performance in a similar situation in the future?

Self-assessment

Think about your performance on the tasks. Were you able to:

- prepare an action plan?   ☐ yes   ☐ need more practice
- hold a crisis meeting?   ☐ yes   ☐ need more practice

Unit 10 ■ 51

Unit 11 | Adapt to your audience

| Use informal language | Simplify and explain |

What do you think?
Pairs
10 minutes

Presentation styles

Discuss the situations 1–3 and answer the questions below.

1 An engineer from R&D presents an idea for a new hi-tech product to senior managers. She asks for a budget for product development.
2 During a sales team meeting, a salesperson presents the latest figures for their region.
3 Thirty HR managers from different subsidiaries meet to discuss strategy. The HR Director from head office gives a presentation proposing a new strategy.

a What is the main purpose of each presentation: to inform or to persuade?
b What style of presentation would you give in each case: formal, informal, specialist (using the terms that belong to your professional field) or non-specialist (explaining the subject in simple terms)?
c In which situations could you include some humour?

Good business practice, page 77

CD 20 Listening 1
5 minutes

Listen to two extracts from presentations, both of them about a company's decision to go public, and answer the questions.

1 How would you describe each extract: formal or informal? Give reasons.
2 Who do you think the audience is in each case?

What do you say?
10 minutes

Formal and informal language

Look at the language features 1–6. Then decide if the examples a–e below represent formal or informal language. There may be more than one feature in some examples.

Features of formal language

1 Impersonal (avoiding *I*, *you*, etc.); may use passive verbs
2 Well-constructed grammatical sentences; may be quite complex
3 Formal vocabulary and phrases that express ideas precisely (*therefore, in addition, the majority of, considerably, we propose to,* etc.)

Features of informal language

4 Personal (using *I*, *you*, etc.); using active verb forms
5 Shorter sentences or chunks (meaningful pieces of language that could be a phrase but not a complete sentence); some sentences may be incomplete or ungrammatical
6 Informal vocabulary, colloquial expressions and less precision (*but, what's more, a bit, I want to,* etc.)

a I want to tell you something about our financial situation.
b This is a challenging situation and one that must be carefully considered before any action is decided.
c So, the next slide – have a look at this – the product sales worldwide …
d The aim of this talk is to provide information about the company's financial position over the last five years.
e Although domestic sales have been disappointing in the last year, the international picture is much more encouraging, as can be seen in the next slide.

Grammar reference: Review of tenses 1, The passive, page 83

Task 1
Pairs or small groups

Objective: Use informal language

Choose one of the topics, A or B.

Topic A: A company's management structure, turn to page 101.
Topic B: Prospects for an international engineering firm, turn to page 103.

5 minutes

Step 1 Preparation

Read the formal speech at the back of the book and discuss what it means. You are going to present the same information to a small group in an informal situation. What words or phrases will you change to make the language more informal?

10 minutes

Step 2 Presentation

Present the information in informal language to another pair or group. Listen to the other speakers and make a note of *three* examples of informal language that they use. Refer to the list of points in *What do you say?* above.

Analysis
5 minutes

Was it easy to follow the meaning?
What examples of informal language did each presenter use?

Unit 11 ■ 53

Culture at work

Giving presentations

For cultures which are substance oriented, the main aim of a presentation is to communicate facts. It is the content of the talk which is important. In style-oriented cultures, presenters are expected to create an impact. Which culture do you belong to? Complete your culture profile on page 82.

	Style-oriented	Substance-oriented
To entertain or not?	Even in formal situations, presentations can be entertaining: the audience will pay more attention.	In business situations, the purpose of a presentation is to inform not to entertain.
Humour	Audiences appreciate jokes and funny stories.	Presenters who try to be funny may lose the respect of their audience.
Pace	Presentations are often fast and dynamic in order to hold the audience's attention.	The pace may be slow to make sure that no one misses any of the points.
Visuals and body language	Presenters use interesting, colourful visuals. They move about when presenting and often make big gestures.	The visuals aren't important provided they are clear and accurate. Presenters generally stand still and don't move their arms or hands much.

CD 21 Listening 2
10 minutes

Fastgro is a company that is expanding rapidly and setting up subsidiaries abroad. The senior managers have invited a management consultant to come and talk to them about how to manage change within the company. Listen to two versions of the consultant's presentation. Which version do you find easier to follow? Give reasons.

What do you say?
5 minutes

Non-specialist presentations

Look at the strategies 1–3 for explaining a specialist subject to a non-expert audience and match them with the phrases a–g below.

1 Simplify the content
2 Reformulate or paraphrase to explain what you have said
3 Give examples or use visuals as support

a Let me put it another way ...
b The following slide illustrates my point.
c In other words ...
d To put it in simple terms ...
e For instance ...
f Don't worry about the details. The important point / main thing is ...
g Let me give you an example ...

Task 2
Pairs or small groups

Objective: Simplify and explain

A consultant is planning a presentation for a non-expert audience and wants to make sure that all the terms and concepts are clear.

15 minutes

Step 1 Preparation

With your partner(s), look at the notes below and discuss how you can simplify or explain the subject matter. Additional information that you can include in your simplified presentation is given on page 103.

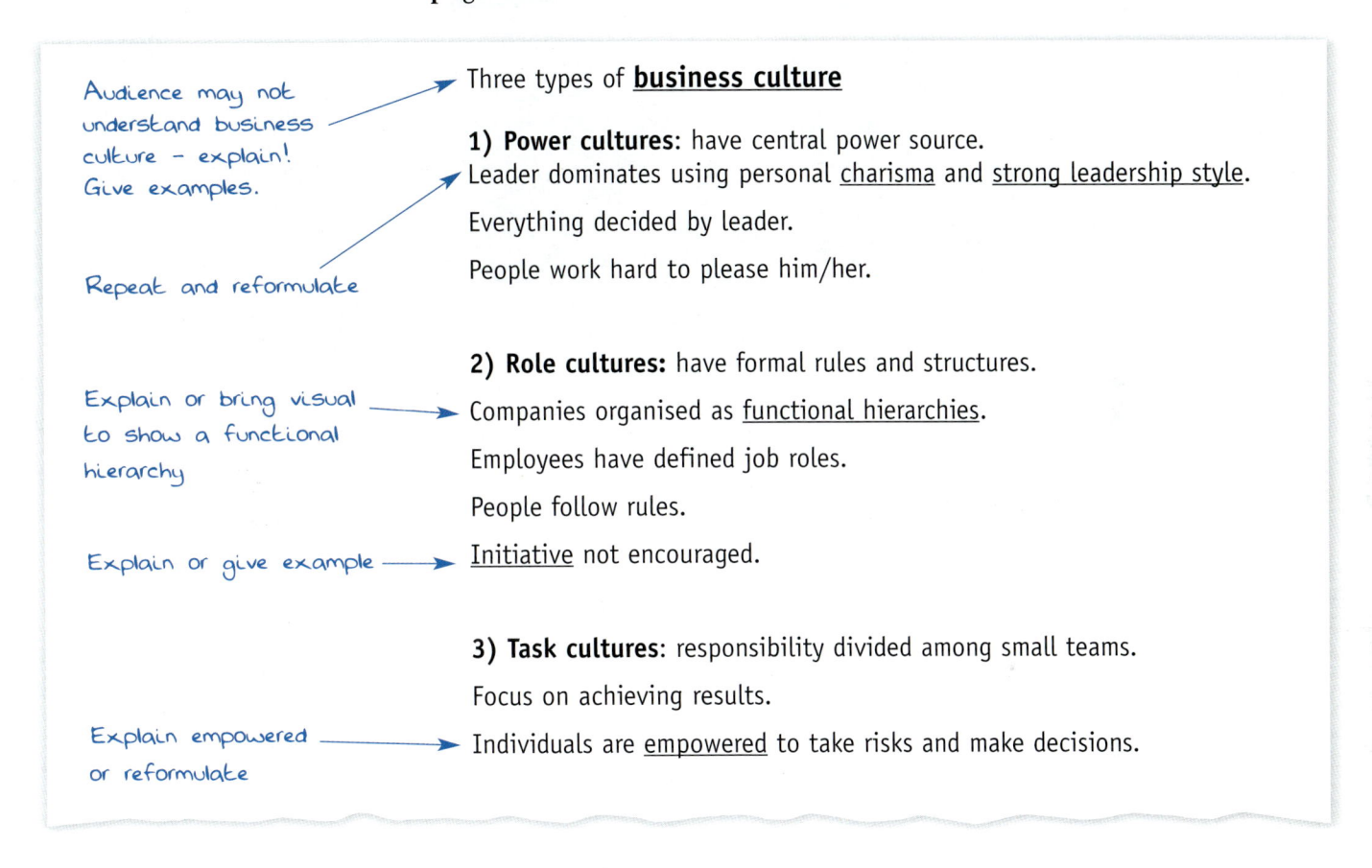

Audience may not understand business culture – explain! Give examples. → Three types of **business culture**

1) Power cultures: have central power source.
Leader dominates using personal <u>charisma</u> and <u>strong leadership style</u>.
Everything decided by leader.

Repeat and reformulate

People work hard to please him/her.

2) Role cultures: have formal rules and structures.

Explain or bring visual to show a functional hierarchy → Companies organised as <u>functional hierarchies</u>.
Employees have defined job roles.
People follow rules.

Explain or give example → <u>Initiative</u> not encouraged.

3) Task cultures: responsibility divided among small teams.
Focus on achieving results.

Explain empowered or reformulate → Individuals are <u>empowered</u> to take risks and make decisions.

5–10 minutes

Step 2 Presentation

One person from each group should present the simplified version.

Analysis
5 minutes

Did the presenter simplify the subject effectively?
Did they use everyday, spoken language?
Did they give explanations of special terms or concepts?
Did they reformulate or paraphrase any parts of the talk?
Did they provide helpful examples or illustrations?

Self-assessment

Think about your performance on the tasks. Were you able to:
- use informal language?   ☐ yes   ☐ need more practice
- simplify and explain?   ☐ yes   ☐ need more practice

Unit 11   55

Unit 12 | Make a difficult call

| Resolve a misunderstanding | Handle conflict |

Strategies for telephoning

What do you think?
Pairs
5 minutes

What things do you find difficult about making a telephone call in English? Discuss the following strategies for telephoning. Which ones do you agree with?

1. Collect together any information and documents that you may need to refer to.
2. Finish the call abruptly.
3. Feel pressured to react quickly.
4. Repeat key information.
5. Speak slowly and clearly.
6. Check that you have understood information correctly.
7. Get annoyed if the other person does not understand what you say.
8. Have a list of key phrases you might need to use in the call.

Good business practice, page 81

Listening
15 minutes

Phillip Davis is a new customer with a broadband Internet Service Provider (ISP). He has a problem with his connection and calls customer services.

CD 22

1 Listen to the conversation and answer the questions.

1. What is the problem?
2. What information does the customer services adviser ask for?
3. Why did the conversation go badly?
4. What could they have done to make the call more successful?

56 ■ Unit 12

CD 23

2 Listen to another version of the call and answer the questions.

1 What question did the customer services adviser ask in order to clarify the number?
2 What two strategies did she use to check that she had understood information correctly?
3 What two things did she offer to do?

What do you say?
10 minutes

Avoiding misunderstandings

Which of the phrases a–h below would you use to do the following?

1 Ask for time (while you look for documents or check information).
2 Check that you have understood important information correctly.
3 Ask for examples or details.
4 Clarify something that you said.

a Can you tell me exactly what happened?
b Just give me a moment ...
c I'll start again ...
d If I understand the situation correctly ...
e Bear with me ...
f I didn't explain that clearly, what I mean is ...
g Could I have ...
h So, what you are saying is ...

Task 1
Pairs
10 minutes

Objective: Resolve a misunderstanding

A customer has a problem with an interactive whiteboard that they have purchased from a mail-order company. The customer's initial call to the customer services department of ActiMedia led to some misunderstandings. Read the information and role-play the next conversation they have.

Student A: You work for customer services at ActiMedia. A colleague asks you to telephone the customer. Use the notes on page 99 to clarify and resolve the problem.

Student B: You are the customer. A different customer services adviser telephones you. Use the notes on page 104 to clarify information and decide what you want ActiMedia to do to resolve the problem.

Analysis
5 minutes

What strategies did you use to avoid misunderstandings?
What course of action did you agree on?

Grammar reference: Future forms, page 85

Grammar reference: Linking ideas 1, Time clauses, page 89

What do you say?
10 minutes

Handling conflict

Match the strategies for handling conflict 1–5 with the phrases a–e.

1. Acknowledge the problem
2. Ask for examples
3. Use positive language
4. Turn a complaint into a request
5. Let the person know that you understand their viewpoint

a. The new deadline is a challenge.
b. Could our departments work together to agree on deadlines?
c. I can see that we need to sort this out.
d. That must have been frustrating.
e. What exactly are your main concerns with the project?

Culture at work

Attitudes to criticism

In a conflict situation, it can be easy for a person from a specific culture to offend someone from a diffuse culture. This is because specific cultures criticise directly. In contrast, diffuse cultures are more likely to want to avoid criticism. How do you handle criticism in your culture? Complete your culture profile on page 82.

Specific cultures	Diffuse cultures
People prefer to get to the point directly. Disagreements are seen as an acceptable way to 'clear the air'.	People take time to get to the point in order to avoid confrontation and 'loss of face'.
Criticism can be seen as constructive – something which can be talked about openly.	Criticism is not seen as constructive and is not discussed openly.
People may use phrases such as *Don't take this personally* before saying something critical, in order to signal that the criticism is not meant as a personal attack.	Criticism may be interpreted as a personal attack however carefully the person being critical words it.
An individual may respond to open criticism by using direct or confrontational language to defend their position.	An individual may respond to open criticism by taking offence and/or withdrawing from the discussion.

| Task 2 | Objective: Handle conflict |

Individually
5–10 minutes

Step 1 Preparation

Hunter Enterprises has recently taken over NaviSat, a small company which produces a high-quality Satellite Navigation System (SNS). In the past, NaviSat did not achieve high sales due to ineffective marketing. Since purchasing the company, Hunter Enterprises has re-branded the SNS and the sales team have successfully promoted the product.

The production team were all originally employed by NaviSat. The sales team are all long-term employees of Hunter Enterprises. The production manager and the sales manager have clashed on a number of issues and it is starting to have a negative effect on the relationship between the sales and production departments. The sales team have just secured a large order to supply the SNS to a shipping company. Instead of being pleased, the production team feel that they were not consulted and that they will be unable to meet the deadline for such a large order.

The production manager and the sales manager are going to have a telephone conversation in order to:

- resolve the immediate problem.
- suggest ways that conflict between their departments could be avoided in the future.
- discuss their respective points of view without blaming the other person.

Prepare for the telephone call.

Student A: You are the production manager, turn to page 101.
Student B: You are the sales manager, turn to page 103.

Pairs
10 minutes

Step 2 Telephone call

Role-play the telephone call between the sales manager and the production manager. Try to use strategies to avoid conflict. Check that you have understood your partner's point of view.

Analysis
5 minutes

What strategies did you use to avoid conflict?
Did you avoid blaming the other manager or department?
How did you check that you had understood your partner's point of view?
If conflict occurred, how did you handle the situation?
Were you able to resolve the immediate problem between the two departments and work out ways to prevent conflict in the future?

Self-assessment

Think about your performance on the tasks. Were you able to:

- resolve a misunderstanding? ☐ yes ☐ need more practice
- handle conflict? ☐ yes ☐ need more practice

Writing 4 — Formal correspondence

| Write a follow-up letter to a telephone call | Write a formal letter |

What do you think? Choose the best answers to complete the quiz about business letters.

1 Experts recommend that letters should use short sentences. More than _____ words in a sentence reduces clarity.
   a) 10   b) 15   c) 25

2 Whenever possible, letters should fit on to _____ side(s) of a standard sheet of paper.
   a) 3   b) 2   c) 1

3 It is not a good idea to include: colloquial expressions, _____ or jargon.
   a) contractions   b) grammar   c) punctuation

4 If you start the letter with a contact name (e.g. *Dear Ms Wells*), then the closing expression used is *Yours sincerely*. If you do not use a contact name (e.g. *Dear Sir or Madam*) the letter ends with:
   a) Yours truly   b) Kind regards   c) Yours faithfully

What do you write?

1 If you deal with a problem on the telephone, it is sometimes necessary to confirm the call in writing. Match the functions 1–5 to the parts a–e of the letter below.

1 Offer further assistance
2 Apologise for the problem
3 Say when you spoke on the telephone
4 Confirm important information agreed in the call
5 Say why you are writing

Dear Mr Cheng

a Further to our telephone conversation on Friday 4 October,
b I am writing concerning the recent problem that you experienced when trying to reserve tickets on our automated booking service.

c As agreed on the telephone, I have now arranged for the tickets to be sent to you by special delivery.

d We are sorry for any inconvenience that this has caused.

e If you require any further help, please let me know.

Yours sincerely

Victoria Saunders

Victoria Saunders, Customer Services Manager

Grammar reference: Reference words, page 92

2 Replace the underlined words or phrases in the letter with the most appropriate alternative below.

a   1 After   2 In addition   3 With reference

b   1 subject   2 regarding   3 apropos

c   1 discussed   2 settled   3 acknowledged

d   1 regret   2 apologise   3 forgive

e   1 like   2 wish   3 need

Task 1

Objective: Write a follow-up letter to a telephone call

You work for ActiMedia (see Unit 12 Task 1). Write a follow-up letter to the customer who had the problem with their whiteboard. Confirm key information and any arrangements agreed in the call. Remember to apologise for any inconvenience to the customer. End the letter politely and offer further assistance if required.

Task 2

Objective: Write a formal letter

Step 1

Write a letter to your partner.

Student A: You work for a charity. Write a formal letter to your partner. Ask their company to donate something to a charity auction (choose a charity and an object). Give a reason why you chose their company.

Student B: You work for a local business. Write a letter to your partner asking them to come and give a talk (choose the subject, location and date). Give the reason why you have chosen them.

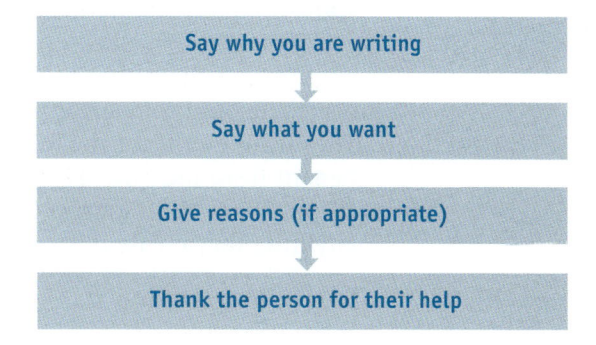

- Say why you are writing
- Say what you want
- Give reasons (if appropriate)
- Thank the person for their help

Step 2

Read your partner's letter and write a response, politely turning down the request.

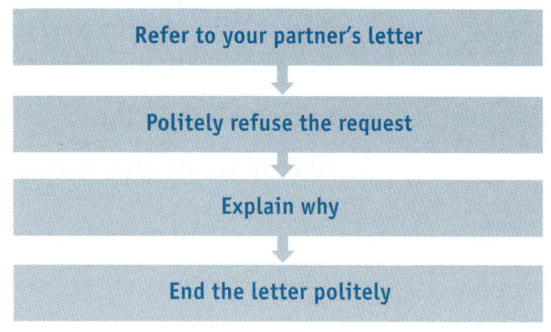

- Refer to your partner's letter
- Politely refuse the request
- Explain why
- End the letter politely

Unit 13 Get to yes

| Make the most of your position | Reach agreement |

Task 1

Objective: Make the most of your position

Two employees of Medilabs, a pharmaceuticals company, have invented a new piece of equipment which has improved production and has reduced the company's manufacturing costs by ten per cent. The company now wants to manufacture the equipment and market it to other pharmaceutical companies. It is a clever invention and could be very profitable. The employees believe that they should have ownership rights because the idea was theirs and they invented it in their own time, not as part of their job. They want credit for the idea (their name on the patent) and a financial benefit from the sales. However, as their employers point out, their employment contract specifically states that the company has full rights to anything they create during their employment.

Pairs
10 minutes

Step 1 Preparation

A date has been set for a negotiation between two of Medilabs' directors and the two employees. Read the information on your role card and work with your partner to prepare your arguments and strategies.

Pair A: You are directors, turn to page 104.
Pair B: You are the employees, turn to page 98.

Groups of 4
15–20 minutes

Step 2 Negotiation

Role-play the negotiation.

Analysis
5 minutes

What was the outcome of your negotiation?
Did the directors or the employees achieve the better result?
Could the directors or employees have achieved a better result if they had tried a different strategy?
Which other strategy could they have tried?

Listening
15 minutes

Two directors of Medilabs meet with the two inventive employees to discuss the future of the invention.

CD 24

1 Listen to part of the negotiation and answer the questions.

1 What was the outcome of this negotiation? Did they find a win–win solution?
2 Who is likely to gain and who to lose in the long term?
3 Which of the strategies a–c did each side use to try to break the deadlock?
   a coercive: explaining the negative outcomes for the other side if they don't agree
   b argumentative: putting forward strong reasons and arguments
   c finding common ground: introducing ideas that the other side can agree with

CD 25

2 Listen to another version of the same negotiation.
What are the answers in this version to questions 1–3 above?
Which of the strategies a–c was the most successful in the end?

What do you think?
Whole group
5 minutes

Negotiating with powerful people

What do you think is the best way to negotiate with someone who has a stronger bargaining position than yourself? Or with someone who is bigger and richer than yourself? Tick the strategies which you would choose. Then discuss your choices with the rest of the group.

1 Threaten them. ☐
2 Let them see that you are in a weak position. ☐
3 Refer to fair standards and fair procedures. ☐
4 Have a good alternative plan in case you can't get them to agree. ☐
5 Offer them something that they want or need. ☐
6 Find examples of similar cases where people in your position have won. ☐
7 Get support from another party (such as a mediator or consultant). ☐

Good business practice, page 79

Grammar reference: Gerunds and infinitives, page 94

What do you say?
5 minutes

Reaching agreement

Match the functions 1–9 with the phrases a–i.

1 Accept that you can't win your case
2 Withdraw from the negotiation
3 Postpone the decision until a later date
4 Signal that you are near to reaching agreement
5 Stress the benefits of finding a solution
6 Ask questions to find out what the other side wants
7 Look for common ground
8 Reach agreement
9 Summarise

a If we can find a way to agree on this, we'll both gain.
b What's the main problem for you? Why do you want to … ?
   Is … important to you?
c Let's go over what we've agreed.
d How can we find a solution to this? Would it help if we … ?
e It seems we're unable to reach agreement so there's no point in continuing.
f OK. We have an agreement.
g I suppose we have no alternative but to agree to your terms.
h We need to take some time to think it over. Maybe we should just leave it for now.
i Look, we've agreed A, B and C. We're close to an agreement. We just need a bit more understanding on …

Culture at work

Negotiating style

In some cultures, people see the world as a battle for power where each individual has to fight to achieve a dominant position. In other cultures, people believe that it is better to cooperate with others in order to find solutions to common problems. Which is closer to your culture? Complete your culture profile on page 82.

Confrontational	Harmonising
People believe they can control things around them by being tough and determined.	People don't believe they can control things outside themselves. They think it is better to accept things the way they are and look for balance and harmony.
People enjoy arguing with others and winning people over to their way of thinking.	People don't like to argue or confront others. They listen to other people's viewpoints and try to be flexible.
Negotiations are about winning or losing. If you get what you want, you win: if you don't, you lose.	Negotiations are about finding a good solution that everyone can be happy with.

Task 2

Objective: Reach agreement

Pairs
10 minutes

Step 1 Preparation

Mogul is an investment bank which employs teams of fund managers, each specialising in a different market sector. It has the following problem.

- The Red Team works in a sector which is booming and has been very profitable in the last two years.
- The Gold Team works in a sector where the profit is small but steady.
- All fund managers are paid bonuses based on the amount of profit their team makes over the year.
- Members of the Red Team have been receiving huge cash bonuses (100 per cent of their basic salary).
- Members of the Gold Team have received only modest bonuses (less than 50 per cent of their basic salary).

Members of the Gold Team feel that the system is unfair. They don't see why they should receive less money just because they work in a different sector. They propose that the profits from both teams are put together and shared out equally. Needless to say, members of the Red Team disagree strongly with this idea.

A date has been set for a meeting between representatives of the two teams and the directors of the company. Read your role card and work with your partner to prepare your arguments and strategies.

Pair A: You are directors, turn to page 101.
Pair B: You are representatives of the Red Team, turn to page 99.
Pair C: You are representatives of the Gold Team, turn to page 103.

Groups of 3–6
15–20 minutes

Step 2 Meeting

Role-play the meeting. A director should act as chairperson.

Analysis
5 minutes

Were you able to reach agreement?
What strategies did each team use?
Which strategy was the most effective?

Self-assessment

Think about your performance on the tasks. Were you able to:
- make the most of your position?   ☐ yes   ☐ need more practice
- reach agreement?   ☐ yes   ☐ need more practice

Unit 13 ■ 65

Unit 14 Sell your idea

| Present a proposal | Make a strong conclusion |

Presenting a proposal

What do you think?
Whole group
5 minutes

1 Imagine you have to make a presentation proposing a course of action to colleagues or managers. Which of the following strategies do you think could help you to convince them?

1 Preparation
   a   Plan to include all the reasons why you want this action.
   b   Find out what your audience is mainly concerned about.

2 Arguments
   a   Prepare as many arguments as you can.
   b   Focus on one or two strong arguments.

3 Presenting your idea
   a   Be clear and specific about what you want.
   b   Make vague, tentative suggestions.

4 Presentation style
   a   Show strong feelings.
   b   Present logical arguments in a calm manner.

5 Conclusion
   a   Prepare a strong conclusion.
   b   Don't worry about the conclusion, just see what comes into your head.

2 Which plan do you think is best for structuring a proposal?

1 Start by stating your proposal, then give the reasons why you need it.
2 Describe the current situation or problem, say what you want to achieve and then lead into your proposal.

Good business practice, page 77

What do you say?
5 minutes

Making a proposal

Look at the steps 1–6 that you might take when presenting a proposal and match them with sentences a–f.

1 Describe the current situation
2 Describe any negative consequences
3 State what you want to achieve
4 Highlight the benefits for others
5 State your proposal
6 Introduce the details of your proposal

a So, what I'd like to propose is a programme of language training for everyone in our team.
b As a result, we often have problems understanding the callers.
c What will this involve? How much will it cost?
d An improvement in skills will be a big advantage for the company because …
e As you know, we frequently deal with phone enquiries from abroad but we don't have adequate language skills.
f If we want to make a big improvement, we need intensive training.

Grammar reference: Linking ideas 2, page 90

CD 26 Listening 1
10 minutes

Sandra Levi is the HR manager in a manufacturing company. Listen to her presenting a proposal to a group of other senior managers in the company and answer the questions.

1 Which structure (a or b in *Good business practice*) does she follow? Do you think this structure is effective?
2 What is Sandra's proposal?
3 What arguments does she give to support her proposal?
4 Does she look at the problem from the employees' point of view or from the company's point of view?

Unit 14 67

Task 1

Objective: Present a proposal

You are going to make the first part of a presentation to colleagues in your department proposing one of the following. (You will prepare the conclusion to your proposal in Task 2.)

1. A two-week language training course in the US for your whole team
2. Flexible working hours for everyone in your department
3. A weekend of team-building activities (camping and climbing) in the mountains for you and your colleagues

Pairs
15 minutes

Step 1 Preparation

With your partner, prepare some arguments to include in your presentation. Decide which of the structures given in *Good business practice* to follow and organise your points accordingly. You don't have to give details of what your proposal would involve. Think about what language you can use to present your points.

Students A and B: Prepare to present proposal 1.
Students C and D: Prepare to present proposal 2.
Students E and F: Prepare to present proposal 3.

Groups of 3
6–10 minutes

Step 2 Presentation

Form groups of people who have each prepared a different proposal. Each person should take between two and three minutes to present their proposal to the others.

Analysis
5 minutes

Which structure did each presenter choose? Was this effective?
Did you find their arguments convincing?
Would company managers give approval, do you think? Why? / Why not?

Culture at work

Showing respect

In some cultures, people are respected according to their status, which is awarded according to seniority, high qualifications and long service. In other cultures, people are awarded respect if they are very successful in their work, even though they may be young and lack qualifications. Which culture do you belong to? Complete your culture profile on page 82.

Status cultures	Achievement cultures
It is disrespectful to criticise high status individuals.	Leaders and managers are open to criticism if they do their job badly.
It is not acceptable for subordinates to make suggestions or proposals to their managers.	Good ideas and suggestions are welcomed from anyone, no matter what their position.
Employees are rewarded in the long term through promotion to more senior positions.	Individuals are rewarded for success in the short term, usually through bonuses and incentive schemes.

CD 27 · Listening 2
10 minutes

Listen to the final part of Sandra's proposal and answer the questions.

1. How does Sandra show that her idea will be successful?
2. Does she use *will* or *would* to describe the outcomes of training? Why?
3. What three benefits to the company does she describe?
4. How does the presentation end?
   a. *Well, that's all I have to say.*
   b. With a repetition of the proposal
   c. With a call for action

What do you say?
5 minutes

Concluding a proposal

Look at the steps 1–4 that will help you to conclude a proposal convincingly. Match each of them with two of the sentences a–h.

1. Give evidence that your idea will work
2. Describe a successful outcome and a bright future
3. Summarise the benefits (ideally, highlight three benefits)
4. End with a call for action

a. The company will benefit because …
b. After the training, people will be able to …
c. The experience of other departments is that we can expect success.
d. I'd like to have your commitment today.
e. Research shows that this kind of training is highly effective.
f. The benefits are less waste, lower costs and greater productivity.
g. If you give your support to this proposal, we can start right away.
h. When we complete this, we'll have more effective procedures.

Task 2

Objective: Make a strong conclusion

Individually
10 minutes

Step 1 Preparation

Go back to the proposal you began in Task 1 and prepare a strong conclusion. Use the language and strategies above. Your conclusion should last one to two minutes.

Groups of 3
3–6 minutes

Step 2 Presentation

Get into your groups from Task 1. Present the conclusion of your proposal to the others in your group.

Analysis
5 minutes

Give feedback to each presenter.
- Was it a strong finish to the proposal?
- Did they convince you that the idea would work?
- What benefits did they describe?
- Was the last sentence positive and encouraging?

Self-assessment

Think about your performance on the tasks. Were you able to:
- present a proposal? ☐ yes ☐ need more practice
- make a strong conclusion? ☐ yes ☐ need more practice

Unit 15 Summarise

| Summarise points | Give an accurate report |

Summarising in meetings

What do you think?
Pairs, whole group
5 minutes

Discuss these questions with a partner and then report your ideas to the rest of the group.

1 Why is it important to have a summary of a meeting?
2 Is it useful to have an oral summary as well as a written record (i.e. the minutes) of the meeting?
3 When is the best time for a chairperson to provide a summary: during the meeting, at the end, or both?
4 What should the chairperson include when summarising?

Good business practice, page 80

Summarising

What do you say?
Individually
5 minutes

Look at the phrases a–g below. Which phrases are useful for:

1 summarising a discussion?
2 summarising information that you have read?

a So, to sum up ...
b This case study is quite long, so let me just give you a brief summary ...
c It says here that ...
d We've discussed the question of ... and it seems that ...
e Some of you think that ... Others are of the opinion that ...
f Basically, the main points in the report are ...
g So, what we've agreed is that ...

Task 1 — **Objective: Summarise points**

Waste Materials Ltd is a medium-sized company that burns chemical waste and recycles it to make new products (such as industrial cleansers). Chemical recycling plants have received a lot of bad publicity lately with environmental groups saying that they produce harmful pollution. The company wants to project the image of a caring, socially responsible and environmentally friendly company.

Small groups
10 minutes

Step 1 Brainstorming meeting

You are senior managers at the company. Hold a meeting to brainstorm ways of improving the company's image within the community where your plant is located. After the meeting, summarise your ideas to the rest of the class.

Groups of 3
15–20 minutes

Step 2 Meeting

The company has decided to use a reserve fund of £100,000 to sponsor a local project that will improve its image in the community. Discuss whether to use the money to sponsor a local nature reserve, provide equipment for a local hospital or provide funding for chemistry research at the local university. Read your information and be ready to summarise the main points for the others.

Student A turn to page 101.
Student B turn to page 102.
Student C turn to page 104.

Groups of 3
5 minutes

Step 3 Summary

After the discussion, one person in each group should summarise the discussion and any decision you reached. The other two should listen carefully and correct or add to the summary if necessary. Make sure that you are all clear about what you discussed.

Analysis
5 minutes

How clearly did each person summarise the written information they had read?
Was your discussion effective? Did you reach a good decision, do you think?
Was the summary of your discussion accurate and clear?

Grammar reference: Reported speech, page 96

Culture at work

Attaining goals in a meeting

Different cultures organise meetings differently. People from monochronic cultures prefer to have a fixed sequence of points and to stick to one topic at a time. People from synchronic cultures may skip from one point to another as related issues are raised. Which culture do you belong to? Complete your culture profile on page 82.

Monochronic	Synchronic
In meetings, it is important to set goals and to follow a logical path in order to reach them.	Meetings have goals, but there is greater flexibility as to how these goals may be reached.
There is a fixed agenda which must be followed exactly. Often a time limit is set for each agenda point.	It is acceptable to deviate from the agenda. Plenty of time is allowed for discussing points not included in the agenda.
The summary and conclusion are important for showing that the meeting has reached its goals.	The most important aspect of a meeting is the sharing of information and opinions. The outcome may be less easy to sum up in a few words.

What do you say?
5 minutes

Reporting what was said

Match the first part of each sentence 1–8 with the second part a–h that goes with it. The linked sentences should make a logical paragraph giving an oral report about a meeting to discuss publicity materials.

1 We discussed ...
2 And we decided to ...
3 We talked ...
4 Several people disagreed ...
5 John pointed out ...
6 Paul felt that ...
7 Catrin suggested ...
8 In the end, we agreed ...

a ... with this idea.
b ... how we could make our publicity materials more exciting.
c ... finding out what it would cost before deciding.
d ... that the costs would be very high.
e ... produce a new brochure.
f ... to postpone the decision until we have more information.
g ... about the possibility of hiring design consultants.
h ... it was more important to have good publicity than to save costs.

| Listening | **Giving an accurate report** |
| 15 minutes | |

Angus, Brenda and Colin, three managers from Waste Materials Ltd, hold a meeting to discuss another PR question.

CD 28

1 Listen to the first extract from the meeting. Make notes on the following points.

1 Do the managers plan to have an open day, an exhibition or both?
2 Who might come to this event?
3 What problem is discussed?
4 What action points are given to: **a** Angus? **b** Brenda?
5 Do they reach a decision at the end of the meeting?

CD 29

2 Listen to Brenda giving a report of the meeting to George, the plant safety officer, and answer the questions.

1 What does Brenda say was decided at the meeting?
2 What does she say will happen at the open day?
3 Who does she say is going to draw up the guest list?
4 What does she ask George to do?
5 When does she ask him to get it done by?
6 Which of the above points does Brenda report *inaccurately*?
7 Did she omit any important points?

Task 2	**Objective: Give an accurate report**

| Individually | **Step 1 Preparation** |
| 5 minutes | |

What should Brenda have said when reporting the meeting to George? Prepare your own short oral report of the meeting. Use some of the reporting phrases from page 72.

| Pairs | **Step 2 Reporting** |
| 5 minutes | |

Report the meeting to a partner.

Analysis	How clear was your partner's report?
5 minutes	Did they give enough detail? Or too much detail?
	Was it necessary to ask questions to get the information you needed?

Self-assessment	Think about your performance on the tasks. Were you able to:
	– summarise points? ☐ yes ☐ need more practice
	– give an accurate report? ☐ yes ☐ need more practice

Unit 15

Writing 5 | Minutes

| Record key information | Record decisions and actions |

What do you think? Which of the following statements do you agree with? Why?

1 The person who takes the minutes plays a key role in the meeting.
2 When taking minutes at a meeting, you should do the following.
   a Write down everything that is said
   b Record only the information that is important for the future
   c Record any decisions that are taken
   d Write the starting and finishing time of the meeting
   e Write a brief summary of each point
   f Record what action is to be taken and who is responsible for it

Good business practice, page 80

What do you write? Look at the extracts from minutes a–d and decide which parts ...

1 refer to an earlier meeting.
2 record important facts.
3 record opinions.
4 record a decision.
5 highlight action to be taken.

a

The question of whether to hire recruitment consultants was considered. Although costs would be high, some members felt that the experience of a professional firm would be valuable. It was pointed out that, as the project is behind schedule, using consultants would save time. After some discussion, it was agreed that more information was needed before going ahead.

Action: AG to research suitable consultancies and costs and report next meeting.

b

Jack presented the accounts for the last quarter. Key points were:
- income from sales is up 3%
- expenses are also up due to the introduction of colour printing
- profit margin has dropped by 1.5% but the overall picture looks healthy.

c

IMPORTANT Everyone to submit their expenses claims by 19th latest!

d
Minutes of Boreham Investors Group
Friday, 14 March 3pm

Present: AG, BD, FH, JS, PS, TW (Chair)

1 Apologies were received from JK and PHS.
2 Minutes of the previous meeting of 22 January were approved and signed.
3 Matters arising:
   Matters arising were discussed under the appropriate agenda items.
4 BD presented a report on recent stock market trends in key sectors. This was followed by a discussion regarding further investments in each sector.
   Technology sector: The market has been falling with a decrease of 2 per cent over the last week. It was decided that no further investments would be made in this sector at present.

Task 1

Objective: Record key information

CD 30

Listen to two short extracts from meetings and write a minute to summarise each of the points discussed. Only record the key information.

Point 1: Petra reports
Point 2: Rosa reports

Task 2

Objective: Record decisions and actions

CD 31

Listen to two more extracts from meetings and write a minute to summarise the result of the discussions. Only record the decision taken in the meeting and/or the action point.

Point 3: What was agreed?
Point 4: Who should do what?

Task 3

Objective: Record key information, decisions and actions

Minute key information, decisions and action points from the meeting you role-played in Unit 15, Task 1.

Grammar reference: Reported speech, page 96

Good business practice

Socialising

Unit 1 — Making contact and building the relationship

- Be the first to say hello and introduce yourself to others.
- Use eye contact and smiling as your first contact with people.
- Make an effort to remember people's names.
- Be able to tell others what you do in a few short sentences.
- Ask open questions (not questions that can be answered *Yes* or *No*).
- Encourage others to talk more by showing interest.
- Respond positively to what they say.
- Look for common interests, goals and experiences that you can talk about.
- Be tolerant of other people's beliefs if they differ from yours.

Unit 6 — Being a good host

Business entertaining often involves interacting with people that we do not know well. A good host makes guests feel relaxed and welcome by anticipating what they need to feel comfortable and helping to avoid what might make them feel uncomfortable.

It is a good idea to:
- welcome guests personally and ask if they need anything (food, drink?).
- avoid being too familiar. It is not a good idea to shorten names or use nicknames unless invited to do so.
- encourage, but don't force, guests to participate in conversation.
- be good company, which means being a good listener as well as a good talker.
- move the conversation away from controversial subjects or areas that might make guests uncomfortable.
- research the cultural background of guests to check what their expectations will be.
- be tactful. For example, if a guest makes a mistake or is unsure what to do, do not draw attention to the situation. Instead, help them to deal with the problem as quickly as possible without embarrassment.

Presentations

Unit 2 — Starting a presentation

Your presentation will only be successful if your audience receives the message you want to give. How well they receive your message depends on a number of factors.

Before you start
- Make sure you are clear about your goals and what you want to say.
- Know who your audience are and what they need to know.

In your introduction
- Say who you are (if the audience doesn't know you).
- Prepare the audience: give the topic and a menu of main points.
- Explain why your presentation is important or relevant.
- Make a good impression (the first 30 seconds are vital!)
  - Make eye contact with the audience before you speak.
  - Be sure to look and sound confident.
- Get attention: make sure your audience listens to you!

Unit 5 — Presenting figures

Spoken information
- Adapt your presentation to suit the audience. Will you need to explain or analyse what the figures mean? Will they need the information explained in simpler terms?
- The same data can be presented in a favourable or unfavourable light depending on how you handle the figures.
- Repeat key numbers in different ways (*1 in 3 people, that's 33%; 175, that's one, seven, five*).

Visual information
- Use visual aids to highlight key information and to support what you say.
- Visual aids increase audience attention and comprehension and help them to remember key facts.
- Don't try to include too much information on a slide. Focus on key data.
- Give the audience a handout to reinforce key information or data.

Unit 11 — Presentation styles

Choosing an appropriate style depends on the purpose, the situation and the audience.

Formal presentations
Large audiences; people from outside your company; special occasions
- Use formal language.
- It is sometimes acceptable to read from a script.

Informal presentations
Small audiences; people you know; everyday situations
- Use informal language.
- Speak without a script.

Note: There may be other differences (clothes, humour, etc.) depending on culture.

Specialist presentations
(expert audience)
- Use specialist terms and common abbreviations belonging to the area of expertise.
- Express your ideas and concepts in precise terms.

Non-specialist presentations
(non-expert audience)
- Avoid specialist terms and abbreviations unless you explain them.
- Express your ideas and concepts in general terms.

Note: Some presentations may be both non-specialist and informal. In these cases, you can use an informal or conversational language style and interact with your audience to check understanding.

Unit 14 — Presenting a proposal

- Specify clearly what you want to achieve.
- Be logical and credible.
- Highlight the benefits of your proposal for the company.
- Provide evidence that it will work.
- Focus on the main interests and concerns of the people you want to convince.
- Think about counter-arguments and how you can deal with them.
- Be positive: describe a successful outcome.
- Create a strong conclusion in which you call for action or for a commitment.

Look at these two ways to structure a proposal.
a 1 State your proposal 2 Explain why you need it 3 Highlight the benefits
b 1 Describe the current situation or problem and any negative consequences
   2 State what you want to achieve 3 Outline your proposal

Team building

Unit 3 Team roles

Understanding and identifying team roles is important for building and managing teams effectively. Members of teams need to value and respect each type of role. Individuals benefit from recognising the role they usually play in a team so that they can develop their strengths and use them to make a valuable contribution. Dr Meredith Belbin of Henley Management College has identified three main types of team roles.

Team members who are action-oriented
- have drive and like to see results • are more focused on tasks than on people
- are good at turning ideas into action • are reliable and efficient • deliver on time

Team members who are people-oriented
1 Coordinators: • are confident and clear about goals • are good at delegating actions
 • are good at motivating and involving people • promote effective decision-making
2 Team-workers: • are cooperative, mild and diplomatic • listen to others' opinions
 • try to avoid friction and seek harmony within the team

Team members who are ideas-oriented
- are creative and imaginative • don't always play by the rules • are bored by routines
- have a different way of looking at things • are good at solving difficult problems
- are often not good team players but are valuable when new directions are needed

Negotiating

Unit 4 Asking questions

In a negotiation, it is better not to make any proposals until you have found out as much as possible about what the other side needs and what their priorities are.

To do this, you should ...
- spend more time listening than talking.
- not assume that you know what they want – check!
- ask: *What's important for you? What's most important for you? Why?*
- get more information by asking: *What else is important? Is there anything else?*
- ask for clarification to make sure you have understood.
- ask: *Can you put that another way?* to get new insights.
- use hypothetical questions to introduce new ideas in a gentle non-threatening way.

Unit 7 Bidding and bargaining

If you go into a negotiation with a fixed target in mind, you may get what you want but you could also miss the opportunity to get more. If you start the bidding with a proposal that is too low and your partner readily agrees, you will realise with regret that you could have won a much better deal. But, once you have declared a low target, it will be impossible to raise it.
- Don't aim too low: set a high target.
- Let the other person propose first. Ask: *What do you have in mind?*
- Never accept the first proposal.
- Try to find a range that you can work within.
- Make it clear what is possible and what isn't.
- Give the reasons for any specific demands you make.
- Try to find out as much as you can about the other person's interests and position.
- Bargain about small points first using conditional offers.
- Keep the discussion open so that you can change your mind: never say *Never*!

Unit 13 Negotiating with powerful people

All the following are useful strategies.
- Refer to fair standards and fair procedures.
- Have a good alternative plan in case you can't get them to agree.
- Offer them something that they want or need.
- Find examples of similar cases where people in your position have won.
- Get support from another party (such as a mediator or consultant).

If you negotiate with someone more powerful than yourself, you need to do two things.
1. Protect yourself against making an agreement that is bad for you.
2. Make the most of any points that are in your favour.

A good way to achieve these two things is to consider your BATNA (Best Alternative to a Negotiated Agreement). That means: think carefully about what you will do if you don't reach agreement. Having an attractive BATNA will give you strength and confidence.

To develop your BATNA, do the following.
1. Make a list of all the things you could do if you don't reach agreement (for example: not sell, look for another buyer, etc.).
2. Take the best ideas and develop them further (for example: where to find other buyers, what price you could get).
3. Select your best option.

During the negotiation
1. Consider what the other side's BATNA is likely to be.
2. Tell the other side what your BATNA is if you think it could help your case (for example: *I've already had other offers; there are other suppliers we could use*).

Meetings

Unit 8 Chairing a meeting

Open the meeting
- Summarise the objectives.
- Refer participants to the agenda.

Encourage, but don't force, participation
- Ask general questions to stimulate debate.
- Ask individuals direct questions to find out their views.

Discourage individuals from dominating the proceedings
- Take one of the person's ideas or points and open it up for general discussion.
- Explain that it is important for all participants to have an equal chance to share opinions. Then invite an opinion from another participant.

Deal with negative tactics quickly, before they create a tense atmosphere
- If participants seem aggressive or negative, ask them to explain why.
- Keep calm. Repeat the objective of the meeting and highlight the importance of working together to achieve it.

Keep the discussion relevant
- Discourage private discussions or ask participants to focus on the point being discussed.
- Be firm about time constraints and the agenda point being discussed.

Close the meeting
- Summarise main points and key actions.

Unit 15 Summarising in meetings

Summarising helps to make sure that everyone at the meeting is clear about its purpose, what has been agreed and why. If anybody has missed part of the meeting, or perhaps was inattentive, summaries will provide an overview of the essential points.

During a meeting, the chairperson should do the following.
- Summarise discussions and say what was agreed after each agenda point.
- Make sure that people know what action is to be taken and who is responsible for it.

At the end of a meeting, the chairperson may sum up as follows.
- Refer to the aims of the meeting and whether they have been met.
- Remind people what points have been covered.
- Give priority to the most significant items or decisions.
- Recap the main decisions reached.
- Briefly summarise the discussion leading up to these decisions.
- Ensure that any outstanding items are noted for inclusion at the next meeting.
- Thank people for their contributions.
- Set the time and venue for the next meeting or a follow-up meeting.

Writing 5 Taking the minutes of a meeting

In addition to an oral summary, it is also important to have a written record of a meeting. The main aims are:
1. to help people remember what was discussed and agreed.
2. to provide information for people who could not attend.
3. to have a written record in the event of misunderstandings or disputes.

The minutes should be accurate, clear, concise and unbiased. They should record:
- the time and place of the meeting
- the names of all those who attended
- the names of people who sent apologies because they could not attend
- the items discussed (though not necessarily the details of the discussions)
- all decisions, agreements or appointments made
- action points (actions to be taken), including the date for completing the action and the name of the person responsible for the action.

Power talk

Unit 9 How to sound more powerful

If you want to be a power talker, try doing the following.
- Use positive language for describing outcomes.
  - Use positive words (e.g. *succeed, win, challenge*).
  - Avoid negative words (e.g. *problem, risk, fail*).
  - Use *when* instead of *if* to talk about future success.
  - Avoid using modals of possibility (*may, might, could*); use *will* instead.
- Speak decisively.
  - Avoid giving tentative opinions (e.g. *I think ... , perhaps ... , I'd say ...*).
  - Avoid 'disclaimers' (e.g. *I may be wrong, I don't know much about this*).
- Avoid using phrases such as *I'm sure* and *I'm convinced* – they often suggest that you are not sure / not convinced!
- Get straight to the point and say exactly what you mean.
- Speak without hesitations and unnecessary words.

Managing a crisis

Unit 10 — Dealing with crisis situations

Before a crisis occurs
- Carry out a risk assessment (look at details such as location where the event is going to be held, the time of year it is taking place, whether extra security might be required because famous people are attending, etc.).
- Prepare an action plan with recommendations on how to deal with each potential crisis situation.

During a crisis
- Clarify the most urgent aspects of the problem.
- Discuss how to deal with the crisis and think of solutions.
- Keep calm and make informed decisions.

After the crisis
- Discuss what went wrong and how to stop the problem occurring again.
- Analyse how you and your team dealt with the problem. Could anything be improved?
- Look at the action plan. What worked? What did not work?

Telephoning

Unit 12 — Making a difficult call

Preparation
- Gather together all the facts, information and documents that you might need to refer to during the call.
- Note down the objective of the call and the outcome that you want. Keep focused on this throughout the call.
- Note any phrases and expressions that you might need.

During the call
- If you feel pressurised into reacting quickly, ask for time (*One moment, please*) or say that you will call back later.
- Repeat and reformulate key information to avoid misunderstandings.
- If you repeatedly have a problem understanding the other person or making yourself understood, keep calm and say that you will contact the person by email or fax.

Ending the call
- Offer to confirm information in writing.
- Don't finish the call abruptly. Check if the person needs anything else or thank the person for giving help or information.

Culture profile

Unit 1 Making small talk

Specific — Diffuse

Unit 2 Attitudes to time

Monochronic — Synchronic

Unit 3 Team-working

Individualist — Collectivist

Unit 4 Questioning style

Direct — Indirect

Unit 5 How much detail?

Low context — High context

Unit 6 Ways of telling a story

Topic-centred — Topic-associating

Unit 7 Bargaining

Deal-focused — Relationship-focused

Unit 8 The function of a chairperson

Results-oriented — Consensus-oriented

Unit 9 Showing emotion

Neutral — Affective

Unit 10 Attitudes to risk

High uncertainty avoidance — Low uncertainty avoidance

Unit 11 Giving presentations

Style-oriented — Substance-oriented

Unit 12 Attitudes to criticism

Specific — Diffuse

Unit 13 Negotiating style

Confrontational — Harmonising

Unit 14 Showing respect

Achievement — Status

Unit 15 Attaining goals in a meeting

Monochronic — Synchronic

Grammar reference

Review of tenses 1

The present simple has the following uses.

- regular events and repeated actions
  *He always **works** late on Thursdays.*
- permanent situations
  *They **manufacture** electrical goods.*
- timetables and scheduled events
  *The CEO **arrives** on Friday.*
- newspaper headlines
  *Miramax **signs** deal with Disney.*

The present continuous has the following uses.

- things happening now and changing situations
  *We**'re waiting for** the chairperson to arrive.*
- temporary situations
  *They**'re closing** the staff restaurant for redecoration.*
- future arrangements
  *I**'m signing** the contract next week.*

The passive

The passive has the following uses.

- when the agent is unknown, unimportant or implied
  *The photocopier **is being** repaired.*
- when the agent has already been referred to
  *Julie complained to her boss, so she **was given** a larger office.*
- processes, systems or experiments
  *First, applications **are considered** and then a date **is fixed** for the interviews.*
- report unconfirmed information
  *Several people **are alleged to have been** involved in the scandal.*

Exercises

1 Complete the email with the correct present tense form of the verbs in brackets.

> Hi George
> As you know Alcott and Eves (¹ be) _____ a major player in the events industry – a recent news headline stated 'A&E (² prepare) _____ to go global'. Well, Bev Andrews, their CEO, called me and she (³ request) _____ that you work on A&E's new account. The company (⁴ aim) _____ for a big launch campaign in March. Mike (⁵ inform) _____ me that you (⁶ negotiate) _____ the Kays deal at present. I (⁷ not need) _____ to tell you that this is more important. I (⁸ try) _____ to contact Caroline in Brussels. She can take over the Kays negotiations immediately. Bev (⁹ arrange) _____ a celebration lunch for us to go over the contract. Mike and I (¹⁰ think) _____ this could be the most important contract of your career.

2 Rewrite these sentences using the passive form.

1. Major employer makes 5,000 redundant.
2. The formula was stolen, they claimed.
3. The committee approved the designs.
4. The president was meeting the delegates.
5. We will give you a week to decide.

Key to Exercise 1
1 are 2 prepares 3 is requesting 4 is aiming 5 informs 6 are negotiating 7 don't need 8 am trying 9 is arranging 10 think

Key to Exercise 2
1 5,000 are made redundant by a major employer.
2 It was claimed that the formula had been stolen.
3 The designs were approved by the committee.
4 The delegates were being met by the president.
5 You will be given a week to decide.

Review of tenses 2

The past simple has the following uses.

- finished actions and events
  We **worked** with them for two years.
- definite or finished time periods
  We **met** some useful contacts at the conference last month.

The past continuous has the following uses.

- background information
  Orders **were increasing** and sales **were going up**, so our shareholders were content.
- interrupted actions
  They **were waiting for** Tom when the fire alarm rang.

The present perfect has the following uses.

- changes that affect the present
  The share price **has fallen**.
- situations relating to an unspecified past time
  We **have tried** to form alliances with several companies.
- situations that started in the past and continue
  They **have worked** here since 2005.
- show duration
  He**'s been** the CEO for ten years.

The past perfect has the following uses.

- give explanations about past events
  We were celebrating last night because we**'d signed** the agreement.
- give background information
  We **had** just **arrived** at the hotel when there was a knock at the door.

Exercises

1 Look at the underlined verb phrases. Is the verb form correct? If not, correct it using the past simple, present perfect or past perfect.

Ali: ¹Had you met our new marketing manager yet?

Jan: No, ²has he been with you long?

Ali: Actually, ³he has joined us two months ago.

Jan: Where ⁴has he been before?

Ali: Saunders and Sons. ⁵He'd left when they were taken over.

Mia: Yes, ⁶he has worked for them for 5 years.

Ali: ⁷I've been told ⁸they've been about to promote him.

Jan: Really? So why ⁹has he left?

Mia: Apparently, the new management already ¹⁰have had someone to run the marketing department and so he ¹¹had taken redundancy.

Ali: Yes, we ¹²had been lucky to get him.

2 Complete the story with the correct form of these verbs.

| arrive | run | escape | hear | buy | visit |

Listen to this – I ¹_____ a new client this afternoon. Suddenly, I ²_____ shouting, and people ³_____ around all over the place. It turned out some guy ⁴_____ a pet rat for his son at lunchtime. Shortly before I ⁵_____ , it ⁶_____ . The funny thing is, the company's called Pronto Pest Control!

Key to Exercise 1
1 Have you met 2 correct 3 he joined 4 was he 5 He left 6 he worked 7 correct 8 they'd been 9 did he leave 10 had 11 took 12 were

Key to Exercise 2
1 was visiting / visited 2 heard 3 were running 4 had bought 5 arrived 6 had escaped

Future forms

will + infinitive has the following uses.

- things that are part of a future plan
  *We'll **make** a statement later today.*
- tentative predictions
  *I think the company's shares **will continue** to increase in value.*
- spontaneous decisions or offers
  *I know – I'**ll invest** in that new start-up!*

going to + verb has the following uses.

- personal intentions or predictions
  *She's **going to sell** all her shares and buy bonds instead.*
  *She is **going to see** Dan in Lisbon.*

Modals have the following uses.

- predictions about things that are possible
  *I **may** / **might** / **could** meet you tomorrow.*

(For more on modals see page 86.)

The present simple has the following uses.

- timetabled events
  *The conference **begins** at 9.00am.*
- conditions necessary for a future event to happen
  *If the price **falls** any further, I'll sell.*

The present continuous has the following uses.

- events arranged for a certain time
  *I'**m meeting** the analysts next week.*

The future continuous has the following uses.

- actions in progress at a time in the future
  *In a week's time I'**ll be starting** my new job.*

The future perfect has the following uses.

- things that will take place before something else happens
  *We'**ll have finished** our meeting by the time your presentation starts.*

Exercises

1 Choose the correct future form in italics to complete the sentences.

1 Don't phone me on Friday morning – I'll *be interviewing / have interviewed* till lunchtime.
2 We'll *be spending / have spent* all of our budget before the end of the project.
3 The technical problems will *have been solved / be solving* by the time you start your call.
4 Do you think you'll *have done / be doing* the same job five years from now?
5 She'll *have stayed / be staying* at the Olympia Hotel in a week's time.

2 Change the underlined verb phrases to an appropriate future form where necessary.

1 We'll have to postpone the negotiation – <u>I won't be receiving</u> the documents by the time we are scheduled to meet.
2 Let me check her diary. <u>She'll have been meeting</u> the CEO on Tuesday morning, but she's free all afternoon.
3 In an hour's time, <u>we'll just be arriving</u> at the exhibition hall.
4 It's an excellent product but <u>they won't have made</u> any profit for at least three years because the parts are so expensive.
5 What time <u>will the meeting have started</u>?
6 Head office <u>isn't going to be</u> happy when you tell them that the contract has fallen through.
7 The price of our shares <u>is possibly falling</u> in the next quarter if we don't stop the current decline in productivity.
8 In January of next year <u>I'll be working</u> here for ten years.

Key to Exercise 1
1 be interviewing 2 have spent 3 have been solved 4 be doing 5 be staying

Key to Exercise 2
1 I won't have received
2 She's meeting / She'll be meeting
3 correct (we'll just have arrived is also possible)
4 they won't make / they're not going to make
5 does the meeting start / is the meeting starting / is the meeting going to start
6 correct (won't be happy is also possible)
7 will fall / is possibly going to fall / may fall / might fall / could fall
8 I'll have worked / I'll have been working

Grammar reference ■ 85

Modal forms

Uses of modal forms include the following.

- possibility

  We **may** / **might** / **could** get more people working on the project.

- obligation

  There **must** be good working relationships between team members.

- advice

  The team **should** / **ought to** consider all the options.

- deductions

  positive: *They're not back home yet; they **must** be working late.*

  negative: *He **can't** have received my message; I'd have heard from him by now.*

Past modals have the following uses.

- uncertainty about a past situation

  *The misunderstanding **may have been** / **might have been** / **could have been** caused by a lack of communication.*

- advice about a past situation

  *You **should have** / **ought to have** told us that you needed help.*

- deductions about a past situation

  positive: *The team **must have been** very tired after working all weekend.*

  negative: *They **can't have done** their research properly.*

Note: Some verbs such as *have to* and *need to* are often used like modals, but are regular verbs and so follow regular verb patterns.

- obligation

  We **have to** finish the project by Friday.

- necessity

  He **needs to** use the phone right away.

- absence of obligation

  *The team **doesn't need to** / **doesn't have to** get permission to buy new equipment.*

Exercises

1 Which pairs of sentences have a similar meaning?

1. a Dermot mightn't be on time for the meeting.
   b Dermot could be late for the meeting.
2. a We don't have to discuss the budget with the finance department.
   b We oughtn't discuss the budget with the finance department.
3. a They can't have used any initiative.
   b They mustn't use any initiative.
4. a You need to hurry, the presentation has already started.
   b The presentation has already started, you ought to hurry.
5. a We mustn't forget our main objective.
   b We have to remember our main objective.

2 Complete the sentences with these past modals.

shouldn't have   can't have   ought to have
may have   must have been

1. We _____ asked for an extension to the deadline. Then we wouldn't be overrunning now.
2. I _____ calculated the figures correctly. They look too high.
3. They _____ agreed to this without checking with me first.
4. The team _____ misunderstood the brief.
5. She _____ pleased to get the contract.

Key to Exercise 2
1 ought to have 2 can't have 3 shouldn't have 4 may have 5 must have been

Key to Exercise 1
1 similar 2 different 3 different 4 similar 5 similar

86 ■ Grammar reference

Question forms

Open questions ask for information. They start with an interrogative word or words (*where, when, who,* etc.).

Where are you from?
What did you think of the presentation?

- If the interrogative is the subject of the question, there is no auxiliary.
  Which company sells most?
- If it is the object, we use an auxiliary.
  Which company do you work for?

Closed questions expect the answer yes or no.

Have you finished installing the software?
No, not yet.

Tag questions are used in the following ways.

- to check information or seek agreement for an opinion (spoken with falling intonation at the end)
  You'll be arriving at midday, won't you?
  This is really complicated, isn't it?
- to ask a genuine question (spoken with rising intonation at the end)
  You're dealing with this, aren't you?
- When both the statement and the tag are in the affirmative, this indicates surprise or interest.
  Oh, you're from Boston, are you? I know it well!

Embedded questions sound more polite. The word order is the same as for statements; there is no auxiliary.

Could you tell me how long it takes to deliver?
(not *Could you tell me how long does it take?*)

- interrogative words are used for open questions
  Do you know how much the software costs?
- *if* or *whether* are used for closed questions
  Do you know if / whether this is right?

Embedded questions are introduced in some of the following ways.

Can/Could you tell me ... ?
Would you mind telling me ... ?
Do you happen to know ... ?
I wonder if/whether you could explain ... ?

Exercises

1 Change the question from closed to open.

Example *Do you live in London?* → *Where do you live?*

1 Is that woman in blue the president?
2 Did they buy the small one because it was cheaper?
3 Did you give your hostess flowers?
4 Does the talk start at 9?

2 Complete each question with a suitable tag to match the meaning in brackets.

1 It's not time to go yet, _____ ? (check information)
2 You'll be talking about IT, _____ ? (show interest)
3 They agreed to back the project, _____ ? (show surprise)
4 You drive a Mercedes, _____ ? (genuine question)
5 We can continue our discussion tomorrow, _____ (seek agreement)

3 Change the direct questions to embedded questions. Start with the phrases in brackets.

1 What time will Hank be back? (Could you tell me ...)
2 How much did you pay for your flight? (Would you mind telling me ...)
3 Who does this case belong to? (Do you know ...)
4 Is there anything you don't like to eat? (Please let me know ...)

Key to Exercise 1
1 Who is that woman in blue?
2 Why did they buy the small one?
3 What did you give your hostess?
4 When / What time does the talk start?

Key to Exercise 2
1 is it 2 will you 3 did they 4 don't you 5 can't we

Key to Exercise 3
1 Could you tell me what time Hank will be back?
2 Would you mind telling me how much you paid for your flight?
3 Do you know who this case belongs to?
4 Please let me know if/whether there is anything you don't like to eat.

Emphasis

Emphasis is placed on key points in the following ways.

- using a signal to introduce what you want to say

  My question is this: are you sure you've thought of everything?

  This is our proposal: we should invest in gold.

  The main problem is we have no capital.

- using a strong or emphatic word or phrase

  It's **essential** to research the market carefully.

  This is of **the utmost** importance.

  That's **exactly** what we want!

- using the full form instead of a contraction

  It **is** going to be a challenge.

  It is **not** enough simply to have an idea.

- stressing key words with your voice, especially
  - to show sequence

    First, we'll see if everyone agrees, **and then** we'll make the decision.

  - to show contrast

    It's not the **cost**, it's the **timescale** I object to.

  (The stressed words are in **bold** in these examples.)

Emphatic sentence structure

- what ... is / are (that)

  What we should do first **is** prepare the plan.

  What research has shown **is that** long-term investment produces positive results.

- it is ... that ...

  It is the price **that** you need to think about.

- inversion after negative sentence openers

  Never have I felt more proud!

  No sooner had we sold the shares **than** the price went up.

  On no account should you give this information to the press.

  Not only is this a great product, **but** it's **also** in big demand.

- inversion after only, rarely, little

  Only in the property market can prices fluctuate so much.

  Rarely does investing in blue-chip companies fail to make money.

  Little did I know that the market was going to take off like this.

Exercises

1 Choose the best word or phrase in brackets to make each sentence more emphatic. Write it in the correct place in the sentence.

1. I agree that it's the best decision. (totally / highly)
2. It is a tricky situation and we need to proceed with care. (outstanding / the utmost)
3. This is a question which we need to address. (complete / fundamental)
4. Now is not the right time to invest. (definitely / significantly)
5. Winning this contract is important. (absolutely / vitally)

2 Rewrite the sentences to make them more emphatic. Use the words in brackets.

Example *We need better customer service.* → *It is better customer service that we need.*

1. It is surprising that nothing has gone wrong. (What ... is ...)
2. He has a great business idea and the funds to develop it. (Not only ... but also)
3. We can arrive at our goal by planning well. (Only)
4. You shouldn't start manufacturing until you have obtained a patent. (On no account)
5. We didn't realise that our competitors were developing the same product. (Little)

Key to Exercise 1
1. I totally agree that it's the best decision.
2. It is a tricky situation and we need to proceed with the utmost care.
3. This is a fundamental question which we need to address.
4. Now is definitely not the right time to invest.
5. Winning this contract is vitally important.

Key to Exercise 2
1. What is surprising is that nothing has gone wrong.
2. Not only does he have a great business idea but also the funds to develop it.
3. Only by planning well can we arrive at our goal.
4. On no account should you start manufacturing until you have obtained a patent.
5. Little did we realise that our competitors were developing the same product.

Linking ideas 1

Relative clauses

Defining relative clauses define or differentiate the person or thing they refer to.

*I'm talking about the phone **that takes photos**.*

- The following relative pronouns are used to introduce a defining relative clause.

  who, that (for people); *which, that* (for things); *whose* (possessive)

- The relative pronoun can be omitted when it is the object of the clause.

  *The scientists (**who/that**) we were working with were highly qualified.*

  *The diagram (**which/that**) you can see here shows the precise figures.*

Non-defining relative clauses add non-essential information to a sentence.

*The phone, **which has been on the market for a month**, is our latest model.*

- The relative pronoun *that* cannot be used in a non-defining relative clause.
- The pronoun can never be omitted.
- We usually use commas to separate the non-defining clause from the rest of the sentence.

Time clauses

Time clauses give information about how long, or when, something happened in the main clause.

- present

  *The markets **send** in information about sales as soon as they **receive / have received** it.*

- past

  *The firm **had** its first major success when it **introduced** disposable pens.*

When a time clause refers to an event that will happen in the future, the verb in the time clause is in the present or present perfect and the verb in the main clause is in the future. (Using the present perfect emphasises the completeness of the action.)

*We'll **call** you as soon as we **get / have got** the results of the survey.*

Exercises

1 Put commas in the sentences where a relative clause is more likely and decide whether to use *that* or *which* or whether either is possible.

1 The number of internet users which/that is growing daily shows no sign of decreasing.
2 He gave me the data which/that I based my decision on.
3 The presentation which/that went on far too long didn't give us any new information.
4 The report which/that I'm working on at the moment is very complex.
5 Ella told us about a new survey which/that she read about recently.
6 The statistics which/that are often wrong suggest that sales may have fallen.

2 Choose the correct linking word(s) in italics.

1 I'll phone you *until / as soon as* we get back.
2 They were giving the presentation *when / once* the power failed.
3 *By the time / Until* we get the exact figures, there's no point in discussing it.
4 He'll make his decision *once / by the time* we have looked at all the data.
5 I want the team briefed *by the time / until* the CEO arrives.

Key to Exercise 1 (most likely)
1 The number of internet users, which is growing daily, shows no sign of decreasing.
2 He gave me the data which/that I based my decision on.
3 The presentation, which went on far too long, didn't give us any new information.
4 The report which/that I'm working on at the moment is very complex.
5 Ella told us about a new survey which/that she read about recently.
6 The statistics, which are often wrong, suggest that sales may have fallen.

Key to Exercise 2
1 as soon as 2 when 3 Until 4 once 5 by the time

Linking ideas 2

The following linking words and phrases introduce clauses (no comma).

- cause: *because, as, since*

  The company will benefit **because** the staff will be more motivated.

- purpose: *in order to, so that*

  In order to improve working conditions, we need to invest in new equipment.

- concession: *although, though*

  Though the budget is tight, we can still afford it.

- contrast: *while, whereas*

  Competitors invested in technology **while** we did not.

- similarity: *as, like*

  We must put more emphasis on training, **as** they do in other companies.

The following linking words and phrases can come at the beginning, in the middle or at the end of a sentence; they are separated by commas.

- consequence: *therefore, consequently, as a result*

  People are working long hours and, **as a result,** they are exhausted.

- contrast: *however, on the other hand, in contrast, in spite of that*

  Our staff have been working overtime for months and, **in spite of that,** we are still behind schedule.

- addition: *in addition, what's more*

  When people are tired, they make mistakes. **In addition,** they suffer more from stress.

- similarity: *similarly, in the same way*

  Time is wasted when communication breaks down and, **similarly,** when meetings go on too long.

Note that these linkers are followed by a noun: *due to, owing to, as a result of, despite, in spite of.*

Despite the high cost, we've decided that the training should go ahead.

The long working hours are not **due to heavy workloads**.

Exercises

1 Complete the sentences with these linking words.

although   in order to   since   so that   whereas

1. _____ it will take more time, I think we should carry out a thorough survey.
2. _____ we need to attract more staff, salaries need to be competitive.
3. We are proposing training for all staff _____ improve efficiency.
4. We need to set up a monitoring system _____ we can check progress.
5. Managers have flexible working hours _____ production staff do not.

2 Choose the correct linking word(s) in italics to complete each sentence.

1. We need to update computers in the accounts department and, *similarly / on the other hand*, in the personnel department.
2. Fosters have updated their technology and, *in spite of that / as a result*, they are more competitive.
3. We are understaffed and, *consequently / in addition*, everyone has to work harder.
4. Last year we were celebrating success: this year, *what's more / in contrast*, we have seen decline.

3 Choose the correct linking word(s) in italics to complete each sentence.

1. *Owing to / Despite* the increase in oil prices, we have to cut back on fuel consumption.
2. *In spite of / Due to* our best efforts, the situation has not improved.
3. I have no doubt that this accident was *as a result of / due to* carelessness.
4. *In spite / Despite* increased interest in our products, sales have remained low.

Key to Exercise 1
1 although 2 since 3 in order to 4 so that 5 whereas

Key to Exercise 2
1 similarly 2 as a result 3 consequently 4 in contrast

Key to Exercise 3
1 Owing to 2 In spite of 3 due to 4 Despite

Articles

The indefinite article has the following uses.

- non-specific singular countable nouns

  Excuse me, I have **a** question.

- Things and people in general terms (definitions, jobs, nationalities)

  Tina is **an** architect. She's **a** Brazilian who lives in New York.

- in certain expressions

  a few, **a** little, **a** great many

The definite article has the following uses.

- nouns already mentioned or specified

  He's preparing for a presentation. **The** presentation will be about ...

- things and people that are unique or one of a kind

  The 2012 Olympics will be profitable for London.

  The CEO wants it to be finished by May.

- categories or groups of things and people

  The mobile phone has changed communications completely.

- the superlative form of adjectives

  The biggest challenge will be stimulating interest in the presentation topic.

No article is needed with the following.

- proper nouns and names

  Heathrow will have to be expanded again before very long.

- plural things and people in general terms and uncountable nouns

  Presentations of this type are generally given by **specialists**.

  Time and **money** are key considerations.

- abstract nouns

  Interest in our industry remains high.

Exercises

1 Decide if these sentences contain mistakes in the use of articles. Correct the mistakes where necessary.

1. A restaurant is closing. Let's have coffee back at the office.
2. Who do you think the audience might be?
3. He's accountant at Morgan Stanley.
4. Sydney Opera House would be a great location for the new ad campaign.
5. The financial report will be with you next week.
6. Experts seem to agree that the energy needs to be saved.
7. Try to make a connection with your audience.
8. I want to focus on a main argument ...

2 Add *a*, *an* or *the* to the sentences where necessary. Not all the sentences require an article.

1. His presentation had strong start.
2. Finnish delegation is arriving this afternoon.
3. There are only few tickets left for the seminar this afternoon.
4. Finance must be an interesting area to work in.
5. Interest has risen in Telecommunications market.
6. I must emphasise importance of this topic.
7. Your presentation must be clear and include all facts.
8. It's American expression.
9. Have you got results of your latest survey?
10. We want explanations not excuses.

Key to Exercise 1

1 The restaurant 2 correct 3 an accountant 4 correct 5 correct 6 agree that energy 7 correct 8 the main argument

Key to Exercise 2

1 a strong 2 The Finnish 3 a few 4 no additional articles required 5 the Telecommunications 6 the importance 7 the facts 8 an American 9 the results 10 no articles required

Reference words

The following are used to refer to previously mentioned words, phrases or ideas.

- the one, the ones

  *We are currently developing a new range of customer investment portfolios. However, we can only offer **the** old **ones** for the moment.*

- such

  *We've had a substantial increase in complaints from our corporate clients recently. We cannot allow **such** a trend to continue.*

- the former, the latter

  *We advised our client to set up businesses in Latin America and East Asia. **The former** has proved to be a great success, whereas **the latter** has resulted in very little profit.*

- this, that, these, those

  *Microfinance institutions (MFIs) lend sums of money to people in developing countries with no collateral. **That** may seem very risky, but loans are nearly always repaid.*

  *The banking sector has four main types of institution: **these** include central and commercial banks.*

The ones can have the same meaning as *those*, but is generally used in spoken English and in less formal written English.

*Where are the figures? You know, **the ones** we need to show to our client.*

Exercises

1 What do the words in italics refer to?

Memo: All buying department personnel

Our customer liaison unit recently conducted a survey into customer satisfaction and found that there had been a significant increase in complaints. ¹*This* allows us to focus on particular areas that customers are unhappy with and provides us with valuable information. Although a number of areas were highlighted, it appears that delivery times and quality of materials are the two main problems.

²*The former* was largely due to the relocation of warehouse facilities and has now been resolved; ³*the latter* is more complex and will require urgent discussions of supplier contracts. ⁴*These* will take place over the next two to three weeks.

Key personnel in the buying department may be required to attend emergency meetings or to rearrange existing schedules. ⁵*Such disruption* will be kept to a minimum.

Thank you for your co-operation in this matter.

Key to Exercise 1

1 This = the survey (+ what we found out)
2 The former = delivery times
3 the latter = quality of materials
4 These = discussions
5 Such disruption = disruption caused by emergency meetings and rearrangement of existing schedules

Adjectives and adverbs

Adjectives can be used

- before nouns

  It was an **interesting** and **exciting** meeting.

- after stative verbs such as *be, appear, look, feel, remain,* etc.

  I'm **interested** in and **excited** about the brand.

Adjectives ending in *-ing* describe what things are like and the effect they have on people.

Adjectives ending in *-ed* describe how we feel.

Adjectives are often made from nouns or verbs by adding a suffix.

profit – **profitable**   compete – **competitive**
economy – **economic**   ambition – **ambitious**

Sometimes an adjective collocates with a noun to form a common expression.

We had a **lively debate**.
It's a **leading brand**.

Adverbs can be used

- after verbs

  The meeting **rapidly** deteriorated into an argument.

- before an adjective or another adverb, as a modifier

  She's an **extremely** effective chairperson.
  The video-conference worked **really** well.

- before past participle adjectives to show how something is done

  Well-run meetings generally finish on time.

Some adverbs have irregular forms: *well, hard, fast, early, late*.

Adverbs cannot be formed from adjectives ending in *-ly*, for example *friendly, lively, silly, lovely*. A phrase such as *in a … way* is used instead.

Clients are always greeted **in a friendly way** and made to feel at home.

Exercises

1 Choose the correct adjective or adverb in italics to complete the email.

Hi Gerald
Thought you'd like to hear about our planning meeting yesterday. At first the meeting was quite ¹*bored / boringly / boring* but then Kjeld from the Copenhagen office arrived. He was ²*interestingly / interested / interesting* in the relocation plans, but Monique insisted that the information was ³*confident / confidentially / confidential*. They started having a ⁴*live / alive / lively* discussion that soon became a ⁵*heating / heated / heatedly* argument. It wasn't a very ⁶*produced / productive / productively* way to spend the entire meeting. Perhaps Monique reacted too ⁷*strong / stronger / strongly* to the situation. A more ⁸*diplomatic / diplomatically / diplomat* response might have worked better.

2 Correct the mistakes in each sentence.

1. We've been terrible busy for the last two weeks.
2. It was a meeting remarkably interesting.
3. It's usual the chairperson who opens the meeting.
4. It was a hardly lesson to learn.
5. The ideas were unimaginative and totally bored.
6. That idea is complete brilliant!

Key to Exercise 1
1 boring 2 interested 3 confidential 4 lively 5 heated 6 productive 7 strongly 8 diplomatic

Key to Exercise 2
1 We've been terribly busy …
2 It was a remarkably interesting meeting.
3 It's usually the chairperson …
4 It was a hard lesson to learn.
5 … and totally boring.
6 That idea is completely brilliant!

Grammar reference

Gerunds and infinitives

Gerunds have the following uses.

- after prepositions, e.g. *before, after, without*
  Before **rejecting** our offer, consider the alternatives.
- as a noun
  Finding the right solution is never easy.
- after certain expressions, e.g. *it's no use, it's no good, have difficulty, be used to, look forward to*
  It's no good trying to sell it now.
- after certain verbs, e.g. *admit, avoid, consider, deny, (dis)like, enjoy, risk, start, finish*
  I can't **risk losing** my job.
- after certain verbs / adjectives + preposition
  We **believe in offering** good service.
  We're **interested in extending** the contract.
- in some suggestions
  How about meeting tomorrow?
  I **suggest adding** a clause to the contract.

Infinitives have the following uses.

- to show purpose
  Let's shake hands **to show** that we agree.
  Our goal / aim / objective is **to get** results.
- after certain adjectives, e.g. *(un)able, difficult, easy, happy, surprised, (un)willing*
  We're **unable to reach** agreement.
- after certain verbs, e.g. *afford, agree, arrange, choose, decide, demand, expect, fail, hope, manage, need, offer, plan, promise, threaten, would like*
  We've **decided** not **to accept** your offer.
- after certain verbs + object, e.g. *advise, allow, ask, cause, enable, help, invite, persuade, remind, trust, urge, warn, would like*
  I strongly **advise you to consider** this option.
- after certain nouns, e.g. *attempt, chance, effort, failure, need, opportunity, reason*
  We must make **an effort to solve** the problem.

Verbs like *begin, continue, intend, start* can be followed by either a gerund or an infinitive with no difference in meaning.

Verbs like *stop, remember, try* change their meaning when followed by a gerund or infinitive.
Try increasing your price. (suggestion)
I tried to persuade him, but failed. (= made an attempt)

Exercises

1 Complete the dialogue by writing the verbs in the gerund or infinitive.

A: Steve Drew is determined (¹leave) _____ the company.
B: We've tried hard (²make) _____ him change his mind. But we've been unable (³persuade) _____ him to stay.
A: Did you think about (⁴increase) _____ his salary?
B: Yes, of course, and we even promised (⁵double) _____ his bonuses.
A: You could try (⁶use) _____ coercion. Threaten (⁷take) _____ him to court for breaking his contract.
B: What if he decides (⁸fight) _____ ? We'd risk (⁹lose) _____ a lot of money in legal fees.
A: Well, I'm sure he would be even less keen (¹⁰take) _____ that risk than you would!

2 Complete the email by writing the verbs in the gerund or infinitive.

Subject: Purchase of mixer X471

Dear Peter
Thank you for (¹return) _____ the contract. I am sorry not (²be able) _____ to specify a delivery date yet. We have had a lot of difficulty (³obtain) _____ the correct parts from our suppliers. We are making every effort (⁴get) _____ hold of these parts and our aim is (⁵complete) _____ the work within the next few days. Meanwhile, we would like (⁶set up) _____ a meeting with you (⁷discuss) _____ procedures for testing. Could we suggest (⁸meet) _____ next Friday morning? If this is inconvenient for you, perhaps you would be able (⁹suggest) _____ an alternative time.
I look forward to (¹⁰hear) _____ from you.
Kind regards
Gavin

Key to Exercise 1
1 to leave 2 to make 3 to persuade 4 increasing 5 to double 6 using 7 to take 8 to fight 9 losing 10 to take

Key to Exercise 2
1 returning 2 to be able 3 obtaining 4 to get 5 to complete 6 to set up 7 to discuss 8 meeting 9 to suggest 10 hearing

Conditionals

There are four types of conditional sentence.

Zero conditonal has the following uses.

- cause and effect

  If Opec **increases** production, prices **fall**.

- request action in the event of a likely situation

  Let me know if you **get** any more information.

Type 1 is used to

- predict consequences of likely situations

  We **will** discount the price if you **pay** within two weeks.

Type 2 has the following uses.

- predict consequences of unlikely or hypothetical situations

  If there **was** a delay, **we'd (we would)** have to pay a penalty.

- imagine the effects of unreal or hypothetical situations

  If we **didn't have** our own trucks we **would use** a transport agency.

- in negotiations, make a tentative conditional offer

  If you **were to increase** your order to 200 units, **we could** reduce the price.

Type 3 is used for

- hypothetical situations in the past

  If we **had sent** the goods by air, they **would have received** them on time.

Mixed conditionals (Types 2 and 3)

We **would be** in a better position if we **had accepted** their first offer.

If I **thought** your company wasn't going to be successful, I **would never have invested** money in it.

Words, other than *if*, that introduce a condition: *unless, provided (that), on condition (that)*

We will agree to buy the units **provided that** you can deliver by the 14th.

Unless we hear from them soon, we'll assume they're not interested.

Exercises

1 Choose the correct form of the verbs in italics.

1 If the economy *declines / will decline*, prices fall.
2 We can deliver on time if we *send / will send* the goods by air.
3 If James *was / would be* younger, he would be a good candidate for the post.
4 I *had / would have* attended the conference if I hadn't been so busy.
5 If we *predicted / had predicted* the problem, we might have prevented it.
6 *I'll / I'd* tell you what happened on condition you don't pass it on.
7 We *agree / would agree* to renew the contract provided that the price remained the same.
8 Unless we *increase / will increase* sales, we're going to make a loss.

2 Write conditional sentences with the verbs in the correct form to express the meaning given in brackets at the end.

1 If the weather (be) good, we (sell) more. (cause and effect)
2 We (finish) the work on time if we (recruit) ten more people. (unlikely situation)
3 We (finish) the work on time if we (recruit) ten more people. (analyse the past)
4 If there (be) an alternative method, we (do) it another way. (hypothetical)
5 Please (inform) us immediately if you (change) your mind. (likely situation)
6 If there (be) any more changes to the schedule, we (enforce) the penalty clauses. (unlikely situation)

Key to Exercise 2
1 is ... sell
2 would finish ... recruited
3 would have finished ... had recruited
4 was ... would do
5 inform ... change
6 were ... would enforce

Key to Exercise 1
1 declines 2 send 3 was 4 would have 5 had predicted 6 I'll 7 would agree 8 increase

Reported speech

Speech can be reported using the same tense when the fact is still true or we're reporting soon after the direct speech.

'Jan is leaving in a minute.'
→ She said (that) Jan **is leaving** in a minute.

We often change tense, time and pronouns when reporting speech.

'They **are** auditing the accounts **now**.'
→ She confirmed (that) they **were** auditing the accounts **then**.

'We **will** meet here **tomorrow**.'
→ They agreed (that) **they would meet there the next day**.

'I **haven't met** her.'
→ He told me (that) **he hadn't met** her.

'I **can't** advise **you** about that.'
→ She regretted (that) she **couldn't** advise **us** about that.

Reporting verbs are used in these ways.

- \+ (that) clause, e.g. complain, explain, feel, point out, report, suggest
    'The advice wasn't very helpful.'
    → She **pointed out** (that) the advice wasn't very helpful.

- \+ infinitive, e.g. agree, ask, decide, demand, offer, promise, refuse, want
    'I'll reduce the fees if you like.'
    → He **agreed to reduce** the fees.

- \+ object + infinitive, e.g. advise, ask, instruct, invite, remind, warn
    'You should lower your prices.'
    → They **advised us to lower** our prices.

- \+ gerund, when the subject stays the same, e.g. admit, deny, mention, report, suggest
    'Let's go over the figures again.'
    → He **suggested going** over the figures again.

- when there is a change of subject, we use a (that) clause
    'Why don't you go over the figures again?'
    → He suggested **(that) I go/went** over the figures again.

Speech can also be reported by summarising the gist of what the speaker said.

Jacques stressed the importance of good design.
Gina raised the question of reliability.

Exercises

1 Report each sentence, starting with the phrases in brackets.

1 'The office will be too crowded if we have two more staff.'
(People felt ...)
2 'Can you please take care of the accounts?'
(I've asked Tim ...)
3 'Can you please remember to send your reports in by next Friday?'
(The Chair reminded everybody ...)
4 'We heard the alarm at 10pm last night.'
(Witnesses reported ...)
5 'Would you like to present the figures at the meeting tomorrow?'
(Joy suggested ...)
6 'The engineers haven't repaired the equipment yet.'
(He admitted ...)

2 Choose a reporting verb from the list to report what John said.

deny	offer	ask	agree	refuse

1 'Shall I draw up a list of potential suppliers?'
2 'Why hasn't the project been completed?'
3 'I'm not going to fund your travel expenses.'
4 'I didn't take the documents out of the office.'
5 'You're right – it's too early to decide.'

Key to Exercise 1
1 People felt (that) the office would be too crowded if they had two more staff.
2 I've asked Tim to take care of the accounts.
3 The Chair reminded everybody to send their reports in by the following Friday.
4 Witnesses reported hearing the alarm at 10pm the night before.
5 Joy suggested (that) I present/presented the figures at the meeting the next day.
6 He admitted (that) the engineers hadn't repaired the equipment yet.

Key to Exercise 2
1 John offered to draw up a list of potential suppliers.
2 John asked why the project hadn't been completed.
3 John refused to fund their/my travel expenses.
4 John denied taking the documents out of the office.
5 John agreed that it was too early to decide.

Pairwork

Unit 2 Task 1 Page 10

Topic A

Your presentation is about a project to install a new IT system in your company. You are the head of the IT department and you are presenting to a large group of colleagues from other departments to update them on progress. You will have a question and answer session at the end of the presentation.

Main points you will cover:
- background to the project
- progress to date
- schedule for the remaining work.

Unit 6 Task 1 Page 29

Host

- Check whether your guest needs anything (food? drink?).
- Introduce a suitable topic to start the conversation (use your list from step 1 to help you start).
- If your guest appears uninterested or does not respond, react quickly and move the conversation on to another topic.
- Keep the conversation flowing smoothly.

Unit 7 Task 1 Page 34

Student A: Medea's agent

Use this information to negotiate the advance.

Other pop stars have received advances of $1 million for similar publications recently.

Medea wants at least $1 million. You have agreed with her that you will take no commission if the advance is less than this.

You will receive 40 per cent in commission on any amount above $1 million.

You want a quick deal while Medea is in the news: the public has a short memory!

Write down the size of the advance you hope to agree: $_____.

Don't tell your partner until the Analysis.

Unit 4 Task 2 Page 21

Group A: Infos

Note: Only give information if your partner asks for it specifically!

The company

Founded in 2000 by Dr Werner Schwarz

Based in Vienna, Austria

A small, independent firm employing just nine people

Three highly qualified trainers/researchers

Werner Schwarz

Doctorate in Applied Statistics, University of Vienna

Publications: several papers in the *Journal of Applied Statistics*

Lecturer at University of Vienna from 1990 to 2000

President of the Statistical Society

Training

Courses in statistics and database analysis in English, French and German
- General introduction to database analysis
- Improve your business performance
- Advanced training in database analysis

Can deliver training at your offices / anywhere in the world

Customised courses focus on examples relevant to your business

Can offer ongoing consultancy to follow up the training

Fees: negotiable

Consulting

Collect and analyse your data

High level of expertise

Latest technology

Report in English, French or German

Clients

From the following industries:

Pharmaceuticals, petrochemicals, advertising, food industries

Unit 2　Task 1　Page 10

Topic B

The purpose of your presentation is to give some general information about your company to a small group of visitors from another company. You are Head of Sales and your visitors may be interested in buying some of your company's products. You don't mind if they interrupt you to ask questions.

Main points you will cover:
- brief history of your company
- structure and location of offices
- products
- benefits of choosing your company as a supplier.

Unit 13　Task 1　Page 62

Employees

You want:
- credit as inventors of the equipment.
- a financial interest in the sale (preferably a share in the profit of at least 20 per cent each).
- to keep your jobs, which provide security for you and your families.

Choose *one* of these strategies.

1. Threaten to take legal action. A lawyer has advised you that you may have a case, but it is a risk. It could be very expensive if you lose. You would also lose your jobs. Even if you won, you would still have to find the resources to manufacture and sell the equipment. You have no business expertise and no capital to invest.
2. Point out that the contract is unfair. The new equipment is your idea so you should receive credit for it. You worked on the invention at the weekends, not as part of your job. You have already saved the company money and now the company will profit from the invention. They should recognise your contribution and reward you for it.
3. Look for something that the company wants and use this as a bargaining point

Unit 4　Task 2　Page 21

Group B: Headlamp Inc

Note: Only give information if your partner asks for it specifically!

The company

Based in Boston, USA (with offices in Arizona and Colorado)

75 staff, including 18 fully-qualified trainers

Founded in 1995

Founders: An Huang Dok and Dede Smith, leading experts in database analysis techniques

The people

An Huang Dok: 25 years' experience; author of two books on database analysis

Dede Smith: 5 years' experience at the Statistical Institute; has run projects in different industries: retail, textiles and clothing, telecommunications, electronics, motor industry

Services

Data analysis and consulting

Market and industry research

Seminars

Programmes

Database analysis seminar: 3 days (lectures and case studies)

Public seminars (US only)

Programmes onsite in the client company anywhere in the world

Fees: negotiable

Unit 6　Task 1　Page 29

Guest

- Respond to your host's offer(s).
- Your host will introduce a conversation topic. If you want to continue with the topic, respond and show interest.
- If you don't find the conversation interesting, find a polite way to show that you want to talk about something else or introduce a new topic of your own (use your list from step 1 to help you).

Unit 5 Task 2 Page 27

Student A: Internet use in Vietnam

Location: Southeast Asia

Population 2000	82,852,971
Population breakdown by age	
Under 15	33%
15–64	62%
64+	5%
Population growth 2000–2050	51.07%
Internet users 2000	200,000
Internet users 2005	5,111,240
Growth in internet use 2000–2005	2,455.6%
Total population using the internet	6.2%

Unit 8 Task 2 Page 41

Student A

Meeting 1: You are the chairperson. Deal with any difficult situations or people.

Meeting 2: You are a participant. You are bored and do not want to participate.

Meeting 3: You are a participant. Be negative about other people's suggestions.

Meeting 4: You are a participant. Respond normally and give your own opinions.

Unit 9 Task 2 Page 45

Situation 1

Points you could include in your argument.

- Safe investments give poor returns (3–5 per cent at most)
- High-risk investments could pay back 200–300 per cent!
- Only investing in safe markets means no hope of making big money
- We can afford to risk a small percentage of the funds
- Need a balanced portfolio (mix of high-risk and low-risk investments)
- Investing in several different markets will spread the risk
- Even if some investments fail, others may do well

Unit 12 Task 1 Page 57

Student A

Read the notes from a colleague and call the customer. Find out what the customer wants and try to resolve the problem.

> Please call 0242 55456
> - Customer says interactive whiteboard not working — when did it stop working?
> - Model number 4P21V? — we don't do this model!
> - Purchased 5 months ago?
> - Whiteboard was dropped? Customer dropped it?
>
> Talk to customer and decide on the best action:
> 1. Customer returns the whiteboard at own cost for repair.
> 2. Give a refund.
> 3. Send a new whiteboard by special delivery (24 hours) — try to avoid this option!

Unit 13 Task 2 Page 65

Representatives of the Red Team

You want to keep the present bonus system, which gives you the opportunity to earn very high bonuses in good years.

Choose *one* of these strategies.

1. Threaten. A reduction in your bonuses could encourage people to look for jobs in other banks.
2. Present arguments to support your case.
   - The people in your team are 'the cream' of the talent within Mogul – you deserve the high bonuses.
   - There is a lot of competition to join your team, which means that the best people are recruited.
3. Look for common ground. There may be ways for the Gold Team to share in the overall profits of the bank without you giving up your high earning potential.

Unit 4 Task 3 Page 23

Supplier

You need to find out about the following.

- The goals of the training
- Number of people to be trained (one course or more than one?)
- Preferred location for the course(s)
- Type of training required:
  - Level / previous experience of trainees?
  - Standard course or customised? (Typical fees: €3,000 per day, standard; €5,000 per day if customised)
  - Length? (usually 1–3 days)
  - To include lectures only (1 day) or practical activities such as case studies (2–3 days)?

Note: Elegante is a subsidiary of Colette, a large multinational retailing and fashion group. Find out if they have their own budget for training or depend on the parent company. Perhaps other companies in the group could be interested in training, too?

Unit 7 Task 1 Page 34

Student B: Publisher's representative

Use this information to negotiate the advance.

Other pop stars have received advances of $1 million for similar publications recently.

Your publishing house has lost two deals recently because the advance you offered was too low. Both books became bestsellers.

You really don't want to lose this deal: you could lose your job as well this time.

Your bosses have said that you can offer as much as $3 million but they don't want to spend more than is absolutely necessary.

The more you save on the advance, the bigger your bonus will be.

You want a quick deal while Medea is in the news: the public has a short memory!

Write down the size of the advance you hope to agree: $_____.

Don't tell your partner until the Analysis.

Unit 5 Task 2 Page 27

Student B: Internet use in Uzbekistan

Location: Central Asia	
Population 2000	26,014,543
Population breakdown by age	
Under 15	37%
15–64	58%
64+	5%
Population growth 2000–2050	96.31%
Internet users 2000	7,500
Internet users 2005	492,000
Growth in internet use 2000–2005	6,460%
Total population using the internet	1.9%

Unit 8 Task 2 Page 41

Student B

Meeting 1: You are a participant. Respond normally and give your own opinions.

Meeting 2: You are the chairperson. Deal with any difficult situations or people.

Meeting 3: You are a participant. Try to dominate the meeting.

Meeting 4: You are a participant. You are bored and do not want to participate.

Unit 9 Task 2 Page 45

Situation 2

Points you could include in your argument.

- Giorgio is a famous chef who will attract lots of customers
- Difficult to find a good chef
- Chefs often don't stay long with the same restaurant; giving Giorgio a share will encourage him to stay long-term
- He will be more motivated to make the restaurant a success
- He will work harder and put more ideas into the business
- Lose him and he will go to work for a competitor

Unit 7 Task 2 Page 37

Student A: Buyer (Smelting Pot plc)

Bargaining points

Payment terms: you want to settle for 30% or at most 35%. You would make a second payment of 30% on implementation and the final payment 3 months (90 days) later. (This delay in making the final payment means you can be sure that the machine is working satisfactorily before you settle.)

You want a warranty period of three years.

Accidental cover is to be included at no extra cost, or at a discount.

As your production process continues throughout the night, you want an after-sales service contract with 24-hour immediate call-out service at no extra cost. (You could agree to a discount.)

Unit 11 Task 1 Page 53

Topic A: Management structure

What I propose to do is to explain the kind of management structure we have established to support the company's operations around the world. It is a style and structure which has proved to be highly successful, and instrumental in our steady growth in the past few years. The company is divided into six profit or business units, which operate completely independently of one another and yet work closely together. The common factor linking all these units is our business strategy, which is critical to our steady growth and ongoing success.

Unit 15 Task 1 Page 71

Student A

> **Charity brings mutual benefits**
>
> There has been a growing trend towards companies and charities collaborating in long-term partnerships. Such partnerships require commitment in ways that go beyond the simply financial. The mining group Larvel Holdings, for example, has spent the last four years working with conservation charity Forest Watch. This successful partnership has included Forest Watch contributing to Larvel's environmental policy and Larvel's staff volunteering to work on the charity's projects. Larvel Holdings confirm that the company's image and reputation have benefited from the link with Forest Watch and that staff involvement in the charity's projects has resulted in improved teamwork skills and increased employee morale.

Unit 13 Task 2 Page 65

Directors

You want:
- all your teams to be motivated to achieve maximum performance.
- bonuses to be largely performance-related.
- your most talented fund managers to stay with the bank.

Choose *one* of these strategies.

1. Keep the present system.
2. Agree to the Gold Team's proposal to share profits equally between teams.
3. Propose a compromise. Part of the profit earned by each team could go into a common fund and be paid out in equal shares to everyone but part of each team's bonus should continue to be related to the team's performance. An alternative proposal could be to offer share options to the teams in addition to cash bonuses.

Unit 12 Task 2 Page 59

Student A: Production Manager

You call the sales manager.

Your main concerns:

- The deadline is in eight weeks. You don't know if your team can meet this deadline.
- You were not consulted before the order was agreed. You want to work out a strategy to make sure that this won't happen again in the future.
- The sales department has already put in another large order for the SNS and you have staff working overtime to fulfil that order (deadline: the end of the month).
- Your staff are not happy about constantly working overtime to meet orders. They are concerned that, in the long term, the quality of the product may suffer. Your team think that the SNS is a great product. You want it to sell well but do not want quality to fall.
- You cannot employ more staff to meet the shipping order as it is highly specialised work and you need skilled staff. It would not be possible to train new employees in time. More employees may be a possibility for the future.

Unit 4 Task 3 Page 23

Elegante Training Manager

Note: Only give information if your partner asks for it specifically!

Mainly sell women's fashions, but also some men's and children's clothing, household goods and cosmetics. No shops or stores: sell online or by direct mail (catalogues).

Goals of training

- Improve business performance
- Target your marketing more effectively
- Gain a better understanding of customer preferences
- Improve customer service

Training requirements

- 10 people working on database management and market research
- Hold training at your own offices in Paris
- Prefer a longer training programme (2 or 3 sessions?)
- Training to include: lectures, case studies (relevant to retail clothing industry) and practical hands-on tasks using own computers and database
- Training and course manual to be in French
- Staff have some knowledge: they need to update and improve their techniques, not start from the beginning

You may be interested in consultancy services as well as training.

You have your own budget (of €20,000) for this training.

You make your own decisions about training and don't have to refer to the parent company.

You don't know anything about the training needs of the Colette group, of which your company is a subsidiary.

Unit 7 Task 2 Page 37

Student B: Supplier (Heath Robinson & Sons)

Bargaining points

Payment terms: you might agree to an advance payment of 35% if you can get an agreement on other points. You would like a second payment of 40% on implementation and a final payment of 20% one month (30 days) later. In your country, it is normal for all payments to be settled within 30 days of completion of a contract. Your finance department would be unwilling to make an exception here.

After-sales service contract: it is very expensive to provide 24-hour immediate call-out service. You could offer some discount on the rate, but not more than 20 per cent.

Unit 8 Task 2 Page 41

Student C

Meeting 1: You are a participant. Try to introduce irrelevant topics.

Meeting 2: You are a participant. Respond normally and give your own opinions.

Meeting 3: You are the chairperson. Deal with any difficult situations or people.

Meeting 4: You are a participant. You feel negative and don't want to be at the meeting because you have a lot of work to do.

Unit 15 Task 1 Page 71

Student B

> The Eastbury Community Hospital is trying to raise funds to replace its ageing CT scanner, which is vital for detecting cancer. According to the Commission for Health Improvement, older scanners do not work efficiently. The recommended maximum age for this type of equipment is seven years and the Eastbury scanner is already ten years old. Theo Cornwall, cancer specialist at Eastbury, said: 'Doctors and nurses are trying to cope with inefficiency and frequent breakdowns and, as a result, patients' health is put at risk.' The hospital is launching an appeal to raise £760,000 for the new scanner. It is hoped that local firms will offer donations.

Unit 11 Task 1 Page 53

Topic B: Prospects for an international engineering firm

We are considered to be one of the world's largest engineering firms. We are currently working on over 100 major projects worldwide, including projects in the chemicals and petroleum sector, hydroelectric power, water management, transport and infrastructure. As a global company, we derive more than 50 per cent of our revenues from projects carried out overseas. We believe that one of our critical competitive advantages is our well-established international network of offices in 30 countries worldwide. Given this global perspective, we believe that the outlook for our business is an optimistic one.

Unit 13 Task 2 Page 65

Representatives of the Gold Team

You want:
- equal opportunity to earn high bonuses.
- the bank to share all profits equally between the teams.

Choose *one* of these strategies.

1. Present arguments to support your case.
   - People in your team have the same qualifications and experience as people in the Red Team and you work just as hard. You therefore deserve a fair reward system.
   - Increasing your rewards will increase your motivation, so you will work harder to achieve success.
2. Threaten. Low bonuses in your sector lead to poor motivation. Good people leave after a short time to join other teams or other banks where they can earn more.
3. Look for common ground. While the earning potential for the Red Team is high in good years, it can crash to zero in bad years. In bad years, some members of the Red Team may even lose their jobs. Your sector is much more stable. Sharing total profits among the teams would reduce the high bonuses for the Red Team in good years but it would have the benefit of reducing their risks in bad years.

Unit 11 Task 2 Page 55

Business culture

Business culture ('the way we do things at work') includes:
- values: what is valued most, e.g. following rules / taking risks?
- attitudes: e.g. towards work: willingness to work overtime
- atmosphere: e.g. stressful or relaxed

Charisma: a powerful, attractive personality; charismatic people greatly influence others

Strong leadership style: not asking for other people's opinions but expecting them to obey

Functional hierarchy: company organised into levels; departments and employees highly specialised; roles clearly defined; authority from top to bottom

Initiative: deciding what action to take without waiting to be told

Empowered: given responsibility to organise own work and make decisions without asking managers

Unit 12 Task 2 Page 59

Student B: Sales Manager

The production manager calls you.

Your main concerns:
- Eight weeks is the standard delivery time for this type of product. You should not need to discuss orders with the production department every time your department agrees to a sale.
- You'd like to solve this problem with the shipping company order before discussing more general problems between your departments. This is a very important client and may result in more sales.

Possible solutions to the problem:
- Production department could employ temporary staff to work on the order.
- Current staff could work overtime.
- Prioritise the shipping order over all other orders. The sales staff could try to extend the agreed delivery time for another large order which is due at the end of the month.

In the future, the production department needs to employ and train more people in order to increase production.

Unit 12　Task 1　Page 57

Student B

Read the notes you made earlier. You receive a call from a different customer services adviser at ActiMedia.
Try to clarify any misunderstandings and check important information.

Product information: ActiMedia Interactive Whiteboard, Model 4VT21P
Purchased 5 days ago.
It was dropped by the delivery people.
After installation it worked at first and then stopped working.
Urgently need new one (giving presentation at end of week)

Note: Office is 120 km from ActiMedia.

Unit 15　Task 1　Page 71

Student C

> The University has a history of successful partnerships with local commercial organisations and can offer many benefits to sponsors. A commitment to support the new research laboratory in the Department of Chemistry, for example, would enable sponsors to display promotional material at conferences held within the University, as well as giving an automatic entitlement to attend graduate recruitment fairs. In addition, the names and company logos of all our sponsors are printed in our annual prospectus.

Unit 8　Task 2　Page 41

Student D

Meeting 1: You are a participant. Try to start a whispered conversation with someone on another topic.

Meeting 2: You are a participant. Be negative about other people's suggestions.

Meeting 3: You are a participant. Respond normally and give your own opinions.

Meeting 4: You are the chairperson. Deal with any difficult situations or people.

Unit 13　Task 1　Page 62

Directors

You want:
- to have control over the development and marketing of the new equipment.
- the company to receive profits from the sale of the equipment.
- to keep the two talented employees in your company.

Choose *one* of these strategies.

1. Stick to your rights. The employment contract gives you full rights to the invention; you don't have to give anything to the employees. However, they may be unhappy with this and decide to leave the company.

2. Negotiate an agreement. You could agree to some of your employees' demands. Propose that you keep control of the product development and sales, but offer some financial benefit in recognition of their achievement (perhaps give them each a one-off payment of €100,000 or a 3–5 per cent share of the profit).

3. Agree that the invention really belongs to the inventor and your employees should, as a matter of principle, have right of ownership. You could suggest that they license the product back to the company to develop and sell. They would be unable to bring it to market on their own, in any case. However, this could lead to other employees demanding the same rights if similar situations arise in the future.

Audioscripts

Unit 1 — Listening 1 page 7 (CD track 2)

1. Can I introduce myself? I'm Narinda Miles from Ryland Finance.
2. There are some very good speakers on the programme this year.
3. Which of the speakers would you recommend?
4. This is a good venue for a conference, isn't it?
5. What did you think of the last seminar?
6. Hi, I'm Mike Lewis. I think I saw you in the presentation this morning.
7. Oh, we're the first!
8. She brought up some interesting points, didn't she?

Unit 1 — Listening 2 page 8 (CD track 3)

Conversation 1
A: Which company do you work for?
B: Oh, it's just a small company. You probably haven't heard of it.

Conversation 2
A: Which talk are you going to this afternoon?
B: Oh, I'm going to one called 'A merger of cultures'. It's especially interesting for me because my company's recently merged with a US company and we're finding that there are quite a lot of differences in the management style.
A: Oh, really? How interesting! What kinds of differences have you noticed?

Conversation 3
A: I see from your badge that you're on the Planning Committee.
B: Yes, I am.
A: And what does that committee do exactly?
B: Oh, just planning next year's expenditure really.

Conversation 4
A: Have you been to this conference before?
B: Oh, yes, several times. I think this one is one of the best, don't you?
A: Well, actually, its my first conference but I'll definitely be here next year.

Conversation 5
A: The food's good, isn't it?
B: Hmm. Yes, it is.
A: Do you know what those things are – the ones that look like little cakes?
B: They're fishcakes. They're quite hot and spicy. Very nice if you like spicy food!
A: I'm not very keen on spicy food.

Conversation 6
A: What kind of job are you in?
B: I'm a geologist. I work for a gold-mining company.
A: Gold mining!
B: Yes, I carry out surveys to find out where the best gold deposits are likely to be …

Unit 2 — Listening 1 page 11 (CD track 4)

Introduction 1

Good morning, everybody. For those of you who don't know me, I'm Wendy Tate and I'm the Project Coordinator for the Quality Standards project which you're all involved in. As you know, the goal of this project is to bring the quality control in all our factories up to the same high standard. We aim to complete the project by the end of June next year, which is a *very* tight schedule, as I'm sure you're aware. We're all going to be working closely together on this. But, as you can see if you look around you, we have people here from several different countries. So it's going to be quite a challenge keeping you all in touch!

So, how can we make sure that the project runs smoothly and finishes on time? Clearly, it's going to be important to establish effective working procedures right from the start. So, what I'd like to do this morning is to go through these and make sure that all of you are clear about them. I'm going to cover three main points. First, I'll give you an overview of the project. Then I'll talk about assessments. And finally, I'll talk about troubleshooting. There'll be plenty of time at the end for you to ask questions.

Right. So, let me start with the overview.

Introduction 2

Presenter: Good morning everybody. My name's Andrew Brent and I've been asked to come along and talk to you today about stress at work and what that means for business.

Let me start by asking you a question. What percentage of employees in the UK do you think suffer from stress? Anyone like to suggest how many?

Speaker 1: Five per cent?

Speaker 2: Ten per cent?

Presenter: In fact, a recent survey in the UK showed that 20 per cent of people suffer from stress at some point in their working lives. That's one in five of all employees. What's more, stress is the second most common cause of absence from work. And the cost of this absence to businesses in the UK is more than three and a half *billion* pounds a year. Clearly this is a huge cost and we, as employers, have to recognise the importance of that.

In my talk this morning, I'd like to cover three main points. Firstly, what stress is and what causes it. Secondly, how we can recognise the symptoms of stress. And thirdly, how we can minimise stress in the workplace.

So, the first point then, what stress is. Stress can be defined as …

Unit 2 Listening 2 page 13 (CD track 5)

Good morning, ladies and gentlemen. I'd like to start by asking you a question. Who do you think has a healthier lifestyle: someone who lives in the suburbs or someone who lives in the city centre? Just put your hands up if you think the person living in the suburbs has the healthier lifestyle. Hmm – that's most of you. Well, it may surprise you to know that, according to research from the US, people who live in city centres are generally healthier than people who live in the suburbs. Why is this? Well, it's because people who live in the suburbs are more dependent on their cars to get around. They walk less, so they are more overweight and have higher blood pressure. We, as planners, need to consider how we can encourage people to walk more.

So, that's the subject of my presentation this morning: 'Planning for healthy living'. I'd like to cover three main points. First: planning for amenities such as shops, schools and sports facilities. Second: public transport. And third: safety – strategies for reducing crime. So, I'll start with the first point, then, which is planning for amenities.

Unit 3 Listening page 16 (CD track 6)

Colin: Well, the situation is this: we can't cover the new order with our existing capacity. So, either we subcontract out to another supplier or we try to handle it ourselves. If we handle it ourselves, we'll have to change over one of the other production lines. Er, Lizzie, how long would it take to make the changeover?

Lizzie: A week at least. I'd really need to have a decision today so we can get started as soon as possible. The production schedule is extremely tight and we'll never meet the delivery dates otherwise.

Tim: But if we change over one of the other production lines, wouldn't that cause problems for the people who are trying to meet other clients' orders? Neil, how would *you* feel if we did that?

Neil: Well, I'm afraid it *would* make it very difficult for me to meet *my* production schedule. Personally, I'd prefer to see the work subcontracted out.

Trisha: I'm not happy about subcontracting. It might be difficult to keep control of quality. And then there's the cost ...

Colin: Quality and cost are indeed big issues. But so is the production schedule. We have to keep in mind that we guarantee on-schedule delivery to *all* our clients. To default on that would be bad for business.

Neil: Why on earth did the salespeople accept such a huge order? They should've realised that we can't possibly deliver it!

Colin: I think we *can* deliver it! This order is a great opportunity for the company and could lead to further business if we get it right. We have to find a way to do this. Come on, everybody. Let's have some ideas.

Trisha: Perhaps there *is* another way to look at this. Does the client need to have the whole order delivered at once? Maybe the sales team could go back to them and see if the deliveries could be staggered a bit? We could deliver in, say, three separate batches.

Colin: Lizzie, do you think you could work out a production schedule if you had a bit more flexibility on delivery dates?

Lizzie: I think it could be done. I'd be willing to give it a try.

Colin: Good. Tim, could you talk to the salespeople and tell them we need a bit of flexibility here? Perhaps they could approach other clients, too, and see where we could gain a bit more time on other orders.

Tim: OK. I'll talk to them.

Colin: Thanks, Tim. And thanks to all of you for your contributions. If everyone pulls together, I'm sure we can do this!

Unit 4 Listening page 22

[RW = Ronald Wheeler; EW = Edwina West]

Extract 1 (CD track 7)

RW: Well, Mrs West, if you don't mind, I'd just like to ask you a few questions about your current security arrangements. It will help me to see what your main needs are so that I can make some proposals.

EW: OK.

RW: So, let's start with your information systems. Am I right in thinking that you don't use any encryption software?

EW: Not at present, no.

RW: Is that something that might be of interest to you?

EW: Yes, I'd like to talk about that, certainly ...

RW: OK, good, we can come back to that. And are you using any software to protect against hackers?

EW: Yes, we are.

RW: What software are you using?

Extract 2 (CD track 8)

RW: OK. Let's move on to talk about your staff. Do all the staff who access the database have a user-ID and password?

EW: Yes, they do.

RW: That's good. Now, I know this isn't an easy question, but would you mind telling me if you use any electronic surveillance to monitor your staff's phone calls or emails?

EW: Absolutely not! We trust our staff. It wouldn't be right to monitor them!

RW: I can understand how you feel. But let me ask you this: how important is it to keep your data files confidential?

EW: It is vitally important. Those files contain a lot of personal and financial information about our clients.

RW: So, if any information from those files was to 'leak out', would that be a fairly serious problem for you?

EW: It would be very serious indeed! If it became known that our client information was not secure, it could destroy the company.

RW: So, what is more important to you: your policy to trust your staff or the need to keep client files absolutely secure?

EW: Well, I suppose ...

Extract 3 (CD track 9)

RW: OK, so we've talked about the supply of security software and surveillance devices. Is there anything else that you feel is important?

EW: I don't know. I think maybe we could use better procedures.

RW: Could you explain that a bit more?

EW: I mean, procedures that our staff could use to keep our data more secure. Perhaps you could advise us on that?

RW: We certainly could. Would it be useful to think about staff training as part of the total package?

EW: That could be useful, yes.

Unit 5 Listening 1 page 24 (CD track 10)

Thanks for coming today. I'd like to brief you on a new business venture that I'm considering. As you know, Kenrig has been doing well in the local South African market, and I'm pleased with sales of all our products. But I was looking closely at the figures for the last quarter and we are now selling seven times more mobile phones than we were in the same period two years ago. That got me thinking. I want to explore the possibility of opening a chain of mobile phone outlets in strategic cities across Africa. So, this is the data-gathering part of the project. I want you to get on to this for me and prepare a short presentation on general mobile phone use in Africa. Jo, as team leader, you can sort out who does what. Then, if it looks as if we should go ahead with the idea, I want you to recommend three countries where we could test run the first outlets. I'd like you to make this a priority, OK? Now, is everybody clear what they have to do?

Unit 5 Listening 2 page 26 (CD track 11)

... and it's the same throughout Mongolia.

Next, I'd like to draw your attention to the recent growth in internet use. Compare these two figures: as you can see, in 2000 there were only around 30,000 internet users. But by 2005 this had grown to 142,000 out of a population of just over two and a half million. This represents a growth of just under 500% from 2000 to 2005. This sounds impressive, but on closer analysis these figures indicate that only about 5% of the total population of Mongolia currently uses the internet.

So, let's move on to the population by age. This chart shows that Mongolia has a relatively youthful population. As much as 95% of the population is under 65. This is significant because we might be able to assume that a younger population would be more likely to use the internet in the future. Look at this diagram to get a better picture of the projected population growth in the 21st century. This data suggests that the population of Mongolia could be as much as four million by 2050. Taking into account the rapid growth of internet use from 2000 to 2005, this means that a large proportion of the growing population could be internet users.

Unit 6 Listening page 30 (CD track 12)

Luke: I hear that you've just come back from the Caribbean, Donna. Well, you've got to hear this story.

Donna: OK. Go on.

Luke: Last year, my brother Joe was at a conference in the Caribbean.

Donna: Was he? Whereabouts?

Luke: Hmm, I think it was St Kitts.

Donna: Ah, yes. I've just come back from St Kitts. It's beautiful.

Luke: Yes, it is, isn't it? Anyway, it was a lovely evening so he decided to go for a walk before dinner.

Donna: Right.

Luke: He'd just started walking in the hotel grounds when, all of a sudden, he heard a shout from near the pool. So, he ran to see what the noise was about, and guess what he saw?

Donna: What?

Luke: There was a woman pointing to a table and screaming. On the tablecloth was a glass, a bottle ... and the most enormous spider Joe had ever seen.

Donna: Eugh!

Luke: Yeah, it was massive, with eight big hairy legs.

Donna: What did he do?

Luke: Well, naturally, Joe didn't want to go anywhere near the thing.

Donna: Sure.

Luke: But he couldn't just run away, so he rushed over to the table, grabbed the glass and put it over the spider.

Donna: How brave!

Luke: Then he quickly wrapped the glass, with the spider in it, and the bottle, in the tablecloth and threw the lot in the pool.

Donna: In the pool!

Luke: Well, what else could he do in the circumstances?

Donna: Right.

Luke: Well, you'll never believe this, the woman started shouting at Joe and then these two men appeared and they started yelling at Joe, too. He was really confused. He was just trying to help out and suddenly everyone's angry with him.

Donna: Why was that?

Luke: It turned out that the woman was an actress. She and the men were from an Italian advertising agency. Apparently, they'd just spent all day filming a TV commercial and Joe had ruined their ad. The spider, which was now very wet, incidentally, wasn't real at all. It was only made of plastic.

Donna: Really?

Luke: Yeah, and I think it'll be a while before Joe tries to be a hero again!

Unit 7 Listening page 36 (CD track 13)

Extract 1

Buyer: We really need to have the new system fully installed, tested and up and running by 1 March. We have big orders to fulfil in the spring, and a new machine is key to improving our productivity.

Supplier: That shouldn't be a problem. Our proposal is to deliver to you by 24 January, which will give us five weeks for installation and testing.

Buyer: Five weeks seems a very short period of time. It doesn't leave any room for error. If there are problems with the installation, we could miss our implementation deadline. We'd like to set an earlier date for delivery.

Supplier: What sort of time were you thinking of?

Buyer: We think 10 January would be reasonable. It would allow two extra weeks for installation and testing – seven weeks in all.

Supplier: I understand your concern. But installation in five weeks is quite normal. We've already allowed time for the correction of any problems.

Buyer: My question is still: can you deliver earlier?

Supplier: It could be difficult. This is a complex piece of equipment and you've asked for a number of modifications. We can't possibly guarantee to have it all ready by the 10th …

Extract 2

Supplier: I have a point to raise about the advance payment.

Buyer: OK.

Supplier: You've proposed an advance payment of 25 per cent of the total cost. However, as you know, we would like to agree a higher percentage to be paid up front.

Buyer: And, as you know, we're not in favour of that!

Supplier: Our problem is, if you want us to deliver before the 24th, this could involve us in extra costs – overtime pay for our workers, for example.

Buyer: Hmm.

Supplier: If you agreed to an advance payment of 50 per cent, we could put that towards our extra costs in delivering a bit earlier …

Buyer: 50 per cent! That's completely against company policy. We've never paid such a huge advance!

Extract 3

Supplier: Well, I've been in touch with our production people and I'm afraid we really can't guarantee delivery by the 10th. However, we think we could deliver by the 17th, giving you an extra week for installation and testing. But we can only do that if you agree to make an advance payment of 40 per cent.

Buyer: Hmm. We want to be absolutely certain that we'll have the machine in operation by 1 March.

Supplier: OK. I can understand your situation. So here's another proposal. To show you how confident we are that we'll complete on time, we're prepared to add a penalty clause to the contract. That means that if there were *any* delay in implementation, we would reduce our price to you.

Buyer: That sounds interesting. Can you be a bit more specific?

Supplier: Well, let's say if there's any delay after 1 March, we would reduce the cost of your total payment by half a per cent per day.

Buyer: Hmm … If you could make that *one* per cent a day, I think we might be able to agree on that …

Unit 8 Listening page 39 (CD track 14)

Meeting 1

Rick: There is no point in going over all this again. There's only one way to approach it.

Sunil: Actually, Rick, I think there might be another way …

Rick: No, Sunil, let me finish. We all know that this is the best way to deal with the problem.

Chair: Thanks for your contribution, Rick, but we need consensus on this. I'd like to hear what other people think. Sunil, what were you saying … ?

Meeting 2

Chair: OK. Any ideas on how we could improve staff morale? OK. Well, if nobody has any better ideas, how about cutting departmental managers' bonuses unless morale improves? Would that work?

Lisa: I'm sure there are other ways to approach this.

Chair: Great. Go on …

Lisa: Umm, well, I think communication problems between departments might contribute to this. I know that a lot of my staff feel frustrated when other departments aren't aware of their deadlines.

Chair: Good. Thanks, Lisa. Roy, does the design team have a similar problem?

Roy: Yes, we do, actually.

Chair: So, how do you think we should approach this?

Roy: Well, perhaps we could have a weekly inter-departmental meeting to discuss key project deadlines.

Chair: Yep, great idea. Paulo, do you agree?

Meeting 3

Sylvie: … so, if we introduce more training seminars, everyone should feel more confident about using the new system.

Frank: Look, this is a complete waste of time. My staff won't accept a new system.

Sylvie: Oh, come on, Frank, if we motivate people and get them on board, there is no reason why it shouldn't work.

Frank: You have no idea what a problem this will be for my department.

Chair: Frank, if I could just come in here a moment. You obviously feel strongly about this. Can you explain why?

Frank: OK. Last year we introduced a whole new system. My staff were unhappy about the change and I worked really hard to convince everyone that it was a good idea, and I'm concerned that it'll de-motivate the team.

Chair: OK, I can understand your concerns now. Thank you for your comments. We'll take them into consideration when we look at how to handle this.

Meeting 4

Chair: Let's look at the visuals for the two designs and see which one we want to go with, OK?

Emma: Oh, look at that colour. Isn't it lovely? That's just the shade I want for my new kitchen, but I'm having a real problem finding it.

Chair: We haven't got much time here, so could everyone who wants to go with design one raise their hands, please? OK, So, how long will it take to make samples?

Emma: I'm really pleased with how the work on my kitchen is going, though. It looks lovely. I've just bought …

Chair: Can I just remind everyone that it is important we keep to the point on this. We've got a lot to get through and time is running out.

Emma: Right, sorry.

Chair: OK, Emma. Now, about those samples …

Unit 9 Listening 1 page 43 (CD track 15)

Jimmy: Well, I think we've got a good product but we can't start the business without funds so, er, I think we should probably go and talk to the bank … see if they'll lend us some money. Then when we've got the money, we can think about how to invest it. We can make decisions about what equipment to buy, and things like that, when we know how much money we've got to invest.

Penny: We have got to get our priorities right. It's no use asking for funding if we don't know how much money we need. What we have to do first is prepare the business plan. It's essential to have a good plan. We need to show investors that we know how to manage a business. The second step is to decide the best type of finance. It's not only banks who provide funding – there are venture capitalists as well. We need to decide our position. How much risk do we want to take? Do we want to keep control of our business? Could we accept a third partner in the business? These are the key questions for us. We must be absolutely sure of our goals before we do anything else.

Unit 9 Listening 2 page 43 (CD track 16)

This is a repeat of Penny's speech from Listening 1.

Unit 9 Listening 3 page 44 (CD track 17)

OK. I've heard your proposal and this is what I think. You have an excellent product here. It's something different, something special. And that's a huge point in your favour. But – and this is a big 'but' – can you sell this product and make a profit? It's the market for the product that's important and at the moment we simply don't know if there is a market out there. As an investor, what I want to know is: who are you planning to sell to? Why will these people want to buy your product? How many people will buy it? And what price will they pay? Market research should be your absolute priority now.

Unit 10 Listening pages 48, 49

1 (CD track 18)

Chair: OK, well, before we move on to the action plan, let's take a moment to sum up some of the potential problem areas we identified in our risk assessment. We brainstormed catering problems and, um, potential transport problems. What else?

Ellen: I've got a note of security issues and fire.

Chair: Yes, and the only other thing is medical emergencies and accidents. That's it. So, shall we start by working out an action plan?

2 (CD track 19)

Chair: … So, shall we start by working out an action plan?

Ellen: It will be the middle of summer and the weather forecast says it will be very hot. So we need to provide lots of shade as it's an outdoor event.

Adi: We could arrange with the hotel to have a couple of rooms available for guests in case they feel ill because of the heat.

Ellen: Yes, and we'll have to tell the catering team to provide water to keep people hydrated. And if food is left out in the heat, it could cause food poisoning. So someone needs to check that.

Chair: Good point.

Ellen: Also, I've spoken to the hotel, and they have medical facilities for minor emergencies and we have eight staff members who have completed first-aid courses.

Adi: The first-aid team could wear special T-shirts so that people can identify them. I'll prepare a list of emergency numbers for local hospitals in case of any major emergencies.

Chair: Great idea. OK, anything else?

Ellen: The hotel has an outdoor swimming pool, which we can use on the day. But they say that it is *our* responsibility to arrange lifeguards. How should we handle that?

Adi: I thought of that, actually, and I've arranged a rota for four members of staff to take turns watching the pool on the day of the party – they're all trained in life saving.

Chair: Thanks, Adi. Ellen, I'd like you to be team coordinator for this. So you will brief the first-aid team, the catering staff and the pool assistants. If anyone thinks of anything else, please speak to Ellen. Right, let's move on …

Unit 11 Listening 1 page 52 (CD track 20)

Extract 1

This morning, we are pleased to announce that it is our intention to make an initial public offering. This offering will comprise 72 million shares of one euro per share, the offer price to be determined by the market. In addition, a total of one million equity shares will be reserved for subscription by employees at the offer price. We estimate that this IPO will reach the market at the end of July, provided that there are no delays in obtaining the …

Extract 2

OK, so I've talked a bit about the IPO and what it will mean for the company and for you, the employees. Now, there's one aspect of this flotation that's especially important for you: *your* right to buy company shares. As you know, the board has reserved one million shares for employees. That means *you* have the opportunity to buy a stake in *your* company. Can I just ask: how many of you have owned shares before? Just put your hands up.

Unit 11 Listening 2 page 54 (CD track 21)

Version 1

Sudden or rapid change can cause a number of problems for an organisation unless the process of change is carefully managed. We can identify four main types of problem: distraction, resistance to change, loss of strategic focus and financial instability. The first problem, distraction, occurs when the focus of attention for managers and employees shifts from efficiency to the process of change. Anxiety about change leads not only to distraction but often, also, to a loss of motivation.

Version 2

As you already know, when a company like yours starts to grow rapidly, it becomes necessary to make a number of changes. For instance, you have to change the organisational structure. You may have to change your management style. This can cause problems if you don't manage change effectively – if you don't carefully control the process of change. I'd like to explain briefly the typical problems you may face in this situation. As you can see here, there are four main kinds of problem. The first one is distraction. What do I mean by 'distraction'? Well, to put it in simple terms, managers and employees can become distracted when they focus more on the process of change than on carrying out their regular work tasks. In other words, they worry more about changes to their work routines than about doing their job efficiently. Let me give you an example. A change in company structure could mean new reporting procedures. Perhaps employees will need to write more reports. Or, instead of just reporting to one manager, they have to report to two or three different people in the organisation. This can cause extra stress for everyone and it easily distracts from the work in hand.

Unit 12 Listening pages 56, 57

[CSA = Customer Services Advisor; PD = Phillip Davis]

1 (CD track 22)

CSA: Good afternoon. Rotel Communications. How can I help?
PD: Yes, I have a problem with my broadband connection. It's …
CSA: Excuse me one moment, sir, can I have your customer account number, please?
PD: What?
CSA: I need your account details before I can deal with your problem.
PD: Oh, for goodness sake!
CSA: Hello? Hello? Is anyone there?
PD: Wait. I can't find it. … OK, it's AC539XM.
CSA: Erm. It's … the account number AC539XN isn't coming up, I'm afraid, sir.
PD: No, not N. M. 9XM.
CSA: Oh, I'm sorry. … Yes, I have your account details now. What seems to be the problem?
PD: Well, it doesn't work. I plug it in and it doesn't come on.
CSA: That doesn't sound like an ISP problem. Um …
PD: So, what are you going to do about it?
CSA: Well, it doesn't really sound like it's anything to do with us …
PD: What do you mean it isn't anything to do with you? I'm paying for broadband and I'm not getting it. How am I supposed to run my business, eh?
CSA: I'm very sorry, sir. There's nothing we can do. It sounds like you need to get your computer checked.
PD: What? What has my computer got to do with anything?
CSA: But you said …
PD: Look, don't try to blame this on my computer. It's down to your inefficient service. I'd like to speak to your supervisor immediately. This is simply not good enough …

2 (CD track 23)

CSA: Good afternoon. Rotel Communications. How can I help?
PD: Yes, I have a problem with my broadband connection. It's …
CSA: Excuse me one moment, sir, can I have your customer account number, please? It will help me to deal with your query more quickly if I can access your account details.
PD: Certainly. Could you give me a moment to find it? OK, it's AC539XM.
CSA: Can I check, that's AC539XN? N for North?
PD: No, it's 9XM. M for Mother.
CSA: Oh, yes. I have your account details now. Would you like to tell me what the problem is?
PD: Well, it doesn't work. When I switch it on, nothing happens.
CSA: Excuse me one second. I want to check that I understand the problem correctly. So, what you're saying is that you switch the computer on and the screen is blank? The computer doesn't come on? Is that right?
PD: No. Sorry, I didn't make myself clear. What I mean is that I turn the computer on, the screen comes up but the broadband doesn't connect.
CSA: Can you tell me exactly what happens?
PD: Sure. I hit the start button. The menu appears on the screen. I try to connect to the internet and an error message comes up.
CSA: OK. Could you tell me what the error message says?
PD: Um, bear with me a moment and I'll check. Yes, it says 'error code 1472'.
CSA: Just one moment and I'll check that for you, sir. … Yes, there does seem to be a problem with the connection. The good news is that we can sort it out immediately.
PD: Excellent.

CSA: Would you like to try to connect while I'm on the line so that I can check that the broadband connection is working for you now?

PD: Thanks, I'd appreciate that. ... Yes, it all seems to be working fine now.

CSA: Great. Would you like me to send you an email to explain what happened?

PD: Yes, please, that would be useful.

CSA: Fine, I'll send that out now. If you have any further problems, don't hesitate to contact us.

PD: Thanks very much for your help.

CSA: My pleasure. Bye.

PD: Goodbye.

Unit 13   Listening page 63

1 (CD track 24)

Employee 1: Look – we worked on this invention during the weekends. It wasn't part of our job to invent new equipment. We believed you would reward us for our good work. Now you want to take all the credit and all the profit. We don't think you have the right.

Director 1: But we do have the right. It's here in your employment contract. Your signatures on this show that you agree to our terms of employment.

Employee 2: You could make an exception. You could agree to the principle that it is *our* invention.

Director 2: Try to see it from our point of view. If we give you the rights to this invention, we'll open the door to all sorts of similar claims.

Director 1: I'm afraid you have no alternative but to accept the company's position on this.

Employee 2: Oh, but we do have an alternative. We can fight you in the law courts. If you can't agree to give us our rights, we'll take legal action. Our lawyer has told us that we have a very good chance of winning.

Director 1: Fine. But if you do that, you risk a long and expensive lawsuit, which could result in your losing everything you own. You'll be putting your families' security at risk. And for what? You don't have the resources to develop the product yourselves.

Director 2: And you don't have the business expertise to take it to market.

Director 1: So, even if you win, you'll be no better off.

Employee 1: It seems we're unable to reach agreement so there's no point in continuing this discussion. You'll be hearing from our lawyers.

2 (CD track 25)

Director 1: I'm afraid you have no alternative but to accept the company's position on this.

Employee 1: We believe there *is* another way to look at it.

Director 1: What other way?

Employee 1: Well, isn't it a benefit to the company to have employees who are creative and innovative? Employees who are contributing to the company's profitability?

Director 2: Yes.

Employee 2: So, you would prefer us to stay with the company?

Director 2: Yes, of course we would.

Employee 1: If you reward us, we'll agree to stay with the company and continue to give you the benefit of our creativity.

Director 1: So, what exactly are you asking for?

Employee 1: All we want is credit for our invention and some financial reward – a share in the profit, perhaps. You'd still have control of the development and a major share in the financial returns. If we can find a way to agree on this, we'll both gain.

Director 2: I think they have a point.

Unit 14   Listening 1 page 67 (CD track 26)

As you know, many people in the company have problems getting their work done in normal working hours. Some people are working a fifty-hour week and, as a result, they are often exhausted and suffer high levels of stress. Are these long hours of work really necessary? I've been looking at the way people work and I've noticed that a great deal of time is being wasted. Time is wasted in meetings that go on too long; time is wasted when colleagues interrupt each other; time is wasted when communication breaks down between teams. So, long working hours are not just due to heavy workloads, they are also due to inefficiency.

This isn't only a problem for employees. It's a problem for the company. When staff are tired, their quality of work suffers and they make more mistakes. What's more, stress is a cause of illness, which can lead to time off work. And stress also leads to low motivation, which can drive people to look for jobs in other companies. All this has a high cost for the company.

If we want to reduce workplace stress and improve motivation, we need to help people reduce their working hours. And the best way to do that is to improve efficiency. We need to show people how to plan and organise their work. We need to give them strategies for prioritising tasks and improving communication. So, what I'd like to propose is training in time management.

Now, what will this training involve? I have here the details of two training programmes that we could consider. The first ...

Unit 14   Listening 2 page 69 (CD track 27)

So, I've given you a breakdown of what the training will involve. What results can we expect? Well, I've looked at some research and there is quite a lot of evidence to show that this kind of training can bring enormous benefits. After just two weeks of training and support, people will be implementing new techniques which could improve their efficiency by as much as 20 per cent. They'll learn to cut out unnecessary tasks that waste time. And they'll work more cooperatively with other team members. There'll be better communication and better coordination of tasks. As a result, people won't need to stay late in the evening to finish their work. The benefits to the company will be increased motivation among staff, less illness and time off work *and* we'll have more efficient and productive workers.

I strongly urge you to consider this proposal today. The sooner we act, the sooner we'll see the results.

Unit 15 Listening page 73

1 (CD track 28)

Angus: I think an open day would be a good idea. We need to show people that we take strict measures to prevent pollution, that our process isn't harmful to health.

Colin: Would people actually *want* to come and look round a chemical plant, Angus? I mean, it's not exactly Disneyland, is it?

Brenda: And do we really want the general public walking all over the plant? What about the safety issues? Personally, I think it would be better to set up an exhibition. We can create models to explain our anti-pollution measures.

Angus: But models by themselves are a bit dull. I think we need to show people the plant as well.

Colin: OK, perhaps we could do both. We show people the models and then take groups round the plant – or parts of the plant.

Brenda: Hmm. I'm still worried about safety. They would have to be quite small groups, I think.

Angus: I agree it would have to be carefully controlled. It would be better if we could limit the number of visitors.

Colin: So, perhaps we should make it by invitation only.

Brenda: Who would we invite?

Angus: Well, the environmental pressure groups for a start. And I think we should invite people whose opinions are important: local government officials, for example. And the media, obviously. Press, TV …

Colin: OK. These are all very good ideas, but I think we need to consider everything carefully before making a final decision. Angus, why don't you make a list of people who could be invited to an open day? And Brenda – could you talk to the plant safety officer? Ask him to do a risk assessment. See if he can do it before we meet again at the end of next week. It doesn't need to be a formal written report at this stage, just a list of some general points for us to think about.

Brenda: OK.

2 (CD track 29)

Brenda: Hello, George. Have you got a minute?

George: Yes, sure, what is it?

Brenda: Colin asked me to come and talk to you. We had a meeting yesterday about PR issues. You know there's all this bad publicity about chemical plants at the moment.

George: Yes.

Brenda: Well, we discussed how we could show people that our plant really is safe and non-polluting. And we've decided to hold an open day. We want to take groups round and show them the plant.

George: What kind of groups? Who's going to come?

Brenda: Well, we discussed the possibility of making it open to the general public, but some of us felt that there could be safety problems.

George: Er, yes …

Brenda: So, we agreed to make it by invitation only. Colin is going to draw up a list of the people we might invite.

George: That sounds sensible.

Brenda: Yes. Anyway, the reason I wanted to talk to you was that we'd like you to do a risk assessment – you know, investigate all the risks so we can see how to minimise them.

George: You want a formal written report?

Brenda: Yes, please. And we need it before the next

Writing 5 Task 1 page 75 (CD track 30)

meeting, which is at the end of next week. Could you do that, do you think?

Point 1

Chair: Petra, can you tell us what the programme is for the Korean visit next week?

Petra: Well, unfortunately, I can't. We've had an email to say that the visit is likely to be postponed by a week or two. Until I know for sure, I can't finalise the programme.

Point 2

Chair: Rosa, how are things going with the preparations for the trade fair?

Rosa: Fine. We're all on schedule. I've been able to book our usual stand by the main entrance, which of course is great for business. The only thing is that costs have gone up astronomically this year. The stand is costing $1,000 more than last year. So, I don't think we'll be able to stay within the budget.

Writing 5 Task 2 page 75 (CD track 31)

Chair: So, we'll need to review the budget?

Rosa: Yes, I'm afraid so.

Point 3

Chair: OK, are we all agreed then? Future committee meetings will be moved to Thursdays to avoid the clash with departmental meetings. Is everyone happy to keep the same start time of 10am?

All: Yes.

Point 4

Chair: We need someone to draw up a new reporting form that will be easier to use. Terry, would you be able to do something about that?

Terry: Er, yes.

Chair: Perhaps you could email a draft to everyone for comments. Then we can agree on a final version at the next meeting.